BRAZILIAN SADDLE SORES

Books by Bruce Vaughan

Juno's Landing
Rabid Dogs in the East

BRAZILIAN SADDLE SORES

Bruce Vaughan

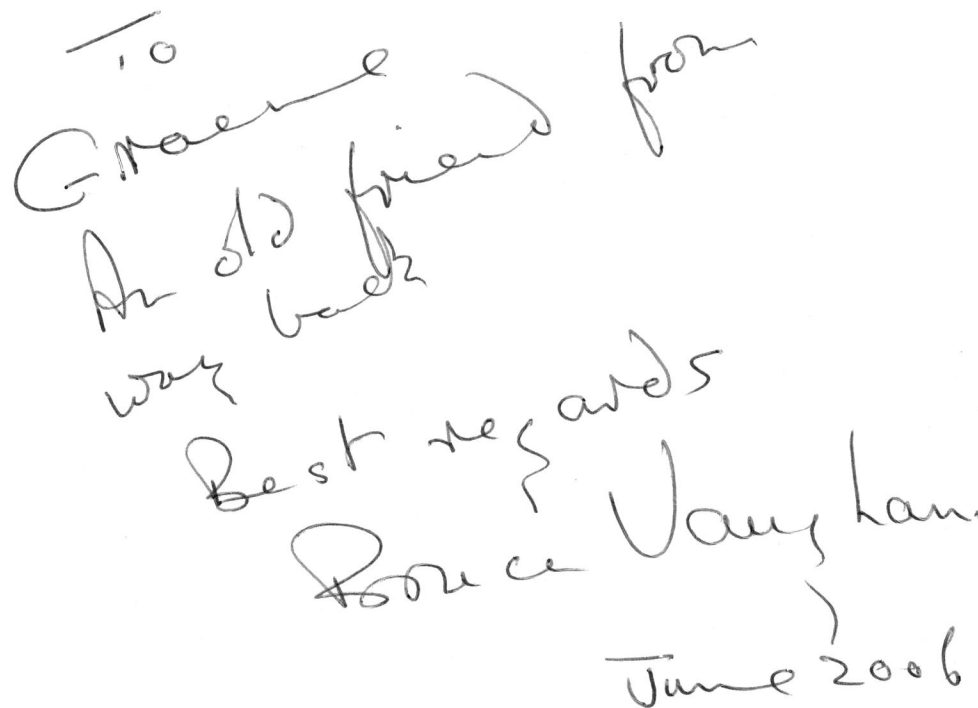

iUniverse, Inc.
New York Lincoln Shanghai

BRAZILIAN SADDLE SORES

All Rights Reserved © 2004 by Bruce Sinclair Vaughan

No part of this book may be reproduced or transmitted in any form or by any means, graphic, electronic, or mechanical, including photocopying, recording, taping, or by any information storage retrieval system, without the written permission of the publisher.

iUniverse, Inc.

For information address:
iUniverse, Inc.
2021 Pine Lake Road, Suite 100
Lincoln, NE 68512
www.iuniverse.com

ISBN: 0-595-32421-5 (pbk)
ISBN: 0-595-77570-5 (cloth)

Printed in the United States of America

Contents

FOREWORD.. ix

Chapter 1	A MEMORY REVISITED..................... 1
Chapter 2	THE UNION COLD STORAGE COMPANY..... 6
Chapter 3	BOUND FOR RIO 11
Chapter 4	DISCOVERING SAO PAULO 14
Chapter 5	STEPPING INTO THE PAST, I GET A HORSE................................ 17
Chapter 6	A MOST UNLIKELY COWBOY 24
Chapter 7	A MAKEE-LEARN VET 30
Chapter 8	A DIFFICULT BIRTH 37
Chapter 9	GETTING TO KNOW THE NEIGHBOURS, CARNIVAL 40
Chapter 10	TRAIL BOSS 49
Chapter 11	FRED 55
Chapter 12	TRANSFER TO MATO GROSSO 61
Chapter 13	LIFE ON THE OPEN RANGE............... 65
Chapter 14	ALONE IN THE WILDS OF BRAZIL 74
Chapter 15	A TRAIN JOURNEY TO REMEMBER 76
Chapter 16	A CUSTOM MADE LASSO 85
Chapter 17	SEBASTIAO, A GRISSLY DISCOVERY........ 88

Chapter 18	THE HORSE RACE	97
Chapter 19	A DEATH IN THE FAMILY, A RIDE THROUGH THE JUNGLE	103
Chapter 20	A WEDDING, NOT MINE AND AN ULCER, MINE	110
Chapter 21	THE IMPORTANCE OF THE FIRST IMPRESSION	116
Chapter 22	A LITTLE TRES BARROS	121
Chapter 23	PEGASUS	128
Chapter 24	THE HOUSE ON THE HILL AND THE JEEP WITH NO SEAT	131
Chapter 25	GONE FISHING	134
Chapter 26	MORE SURGERY, SOME REALTY SAVVY	139
Chapter 27	THE FARMS MANAGER PAYS ME A VISIT	144
Chapter 28	BARRETOS, THE WEIGH MASTER	149
Chapter 29	JACARACATINGA, MY NEMESIS	159
Chapter 30	A WALK IN THE PARK	169
Chapter 31	I DO THE CRIME AND DO THE TIME	173
Chapter 32	END OF AN ERA, SOME SOUL SEARCHING	178
EPILOGUE		185
ABOUT THE AUTHOR		201

ACKNOWLEDGEMENTS

I wish to thank Aileen and Ken Bridgewater for their help, encouragement and guidance in the preparation of the finished MS of this book. A special thanks goes to the people who made my return trip to Brazil so enjoyable, Nick Wykes, David Maklin, Rod Paxton and Elisiario Cleto de Oliveira.

FOREWORD

Bruce Vaughan's book about life on our Brazilian Farms shows a fascinating insight into life there in the 1950's.

It brought back many happy memories for me, as it will to the many people who worked there then.

For those who did not know Brazil then, it is an interesting history of a bygone day.

The farms are still there, but very different.

Fifty years on, life is much easier on the farms, but just as challenging.

I am sure you will enjoy "Brazilian Saddle Sores" as much as I did.

Lord Vestey
Third Baron of Stowell Park

1

A MEMORY REVISITED

It was one of those typical torrid, blast furnace, Mato Grosso days. From the cloudless sky, a relentless, scorching sun beat down onto the sparse, undulating, sandy terrain that reached, interrupted only by occasional poor scrub, to the far horizon in all directions. Dust, stirred into motion by several hundred hooves, turned the sweat patches into mudslides down my face, neck and shirt. A rogue steer had broken from the herd and, wide eyed with fear on finding himself alone, was running towards the sanctity of a scraggy patch of bushes and stunted scrub trees.

My horse knew what to do as soon as I urged him forward, and we galloped to intercept the frightened animal before he reached the cover, where he could get entangled in the thick, coarse and sometimes treacherous undergrowth. I realized that, in spite of our best efforts, I did not have time to cut off the runaway. I had to get a lasso over his head before things got too difficult. I freed the rawhide lasso from the saddle and, without taking my eyes off my quarry, let out a wide loop as I started a slow easy swing. I allowed the heavy ring to slide a few feet away from my hand, to give better momentum for the throw. As the loop swung in a lazy circle over my head, my horse, caught up in the excitement of the chase, focused all his senses as, with ears standing erect, nostrils flared, he quickened his pace, closing the gap.

Horse and rider were both oblivious to the rough, treacherous ground we were crossing; our minds and bodies were in complete unison, we were as one. Our sole objective was to get within range of those horns before their owner reached cover. I was standing in the stirrups, leaning over my horse's head to give me that little extra range. I released the loop at the bottom of the swing and watched as it breached the gap, decreasing in size as it went. Seemingly guided by some homing instinct, the loop, now just three feet in diameter, dropped over the steer's horns. With a quick jerk of the wrist the lasso made fast. At the same moment my horse, with no need for direction from me, stopped in his tracks and made a half turn, bracing himself for the impact. The steer became momentarily airborne and then spun before landing with a thud, half hidden by undergrowth.

As I dismounted and ran towards the steer, I became thankfully aware of the boiadeiros, Brazilian cowboys, coming to my assistance. They positioned their horses to surround the hapless animal, while I grabbed the steer by the nose and horn, forcing his head to the ground. With the steer temporarily immobilized, I released the lasso. Now it was just me against a very angry, scared Zebu steer. I jumped off and ran to the protection of the nearest of the boiadeiros' horse before remounting my own. Still snorting with rage and panic, the steer threw himself towards one of the horses. The rider let him come just close enough before spurring his horse in the direction of the herd, so that the steer followed. The rest of us circled the still snorting, head-tossing animal and, with a little whip cracking persuasion, he was coaxed, at first reluctantly and then happily, back to the herd.

We had been in the saddle since daybreak and still had several hours of trail in front of us before reaching our goal; the loading corral, near the railway station. Our day would not end then. We still had to load the cattle onto the train that was bound for the company's fattening farms in Sao Paulo. It was often an all night job, even when the train was on time, which was rare. All too often we had to hang our hammocks where we could and catch a little steep while we waited.

We arrived at the little railway town of Ribas do Rio Pardo by early evening. The balmy tropical twilight turned the sweltering heat of the day into a surprisingly cool night within minutes. Rio Pardo was a typical Brazilian interior town, more of a village really, and like so many others, it consisted of just one dusty, or muddy in the rainy season, main-street. There were a few simple, mud and timber houses on one side of the street and the raison d'etre, the railway tracks, on the other. The most imposing buildings, and the only ones built of stone, were the station office and platform and the stationmaster's house. Both the important position and the relatively imposing residence gave the stationmaster great social status. The travellers' inn and only restaurant stood across the road from the station. Conrad Hilton would have had no competition in Ribas do Rio Pardo.

"We'll eat first," I announced as we finished the final count before herding the cattle into the corral, "but don't take your boots off. I want to load these gaiolas while we've still got a moon." Much to our surprise and delight, the train, or at least the gaiolas, carriages for the cattle, were there in the siding waiting for us.

After a predictable and yet satisfying meal of gritty, half washed rice, beans and chewy, dried beef, accompanied by the ever present, thick, black, Brazilian coffee, that is constantly on the boil on most stoves, I sat for a while in front of the inn and watched the evening life of Ribas do Rio Pardo. I was twenty-two, going on twenty-three, and had been in the interior of Brazil for nearly two years, yet I felt as if I was almost a Brazilian. I spoke Portuguese with a true Brazilian peasant's accent, with all the right dramatic intonations and hand movements. The cowboys had finally accepted me as one of them. I felt at home and very much a part of this authentic, interior, Wild West setting. The year was 1958.

Forty-two years later I stood once more in the street between the Ribas do Rio Pardo station and the inn, or where it had been. In many ways time had stood still for that small corner of Brazil. The station was still there and so were the houses in the main street, still very similar to the ones I had known however there were some unmistakable changes to the scene. The railway no longer carried passengers and therefore the stations along the narrow gauge railway line, that originated somewhere in Paraguay, had been closed down for many years. The old station building now stands sadly abandoned, dilapidated and forlorn, overgrown with creepers and bushes. Ribas do Rio Pardo, now no longer dependent on the railway for its very existence has turned its back on it. The town, now a sprawling well planned suburbia, has taken on a new, modern life that exists away from the railway line and closer to and more dependant on the new highway that passes a few miles up the hill from the railway. It is now a flourishing, independent little township that has almost forgotten the old main street along the railway track.

Rod Paxton, the present manager of the fazenda that I used to work on, back in the fifties, accompanied me on this little glimpse into the past.

The previous day I had collected my one suitcase at the Campo Grande Airport and headed for the exit; not too sure of what I would find. It had been forty-two years since I had left Mato Grosso and forty years since I had left Brazil, after working for a Brazilian company owned by the British meat conglomerate Vestey.

"Are you Bruce Vaughan?" a very English voice enquired from the sea of Brazilian faces. I looked to see the friendly smile of a man in his fifties. Both hair and beard were greying but the casually dressed body was that of a healthy, active man.

"Yes," I replied, with a degree of relief that must have shown.

"Welcome, I'm Rod Paxton."

This moment was the culmination of two months correspondence that had started with a sudden 'well why not?' notion. I was scheduled to attend a Council meeting in Rio Grande do Sul in April 2000. It was to be my first visit to Brazil since I left in 1960. The idea of revisiting Mato Grosso started off, as I have said with, 'wouldn't it be nice. It's worth a try, well why not,' thoughts, which usually get no further than that. I tried to find the address for Frigorifico Anglo, Vestey's Brazilian company, through the Internet. No amount of searching however could come up with the information that I needed. Eventually, through Nick Wykes, a friend of my brother who had some business dealings with Vestey, I was able to find out that the company had not only moved office from Sao Paulo to San Jose do Rio Preto but had also changed its name from Frigorifico Anglo, to Agropecuaria CFM. I never did find out what CFM stood for. I wrote a letter to David Makin, the General Manager, asking if I might visit one or two of the farms I had worked on. I waited for some weeks without receiving a reply and finally asked Nick Wykes for more advice. His suggestion was to send the letter to the London office and ask that it be included in their courier bag for Brazil. This turned out to be sound advice. I included my e-mail address in the letter and was delighted to find a reply in my inbox ten days later, making me welcome.

The Mato Grosso fazendas and Tres Barros, my first posting, were my first choices for the visit. My time was limited and I also did not want to over stretch my welcome. Fazenda Tres Barros, when I knew it, had been a mixture of citrus and dairy farm. It was a beautiful remnant of the past, having originally been the private estate of a rich landowner dating back to the slave days. I was disappointed to learn that the whole estate had been switched to sugar cane. There had been some confusion during the correspondence about Mato Grosso, as I referred to the fazenda near Campo Grande as Ligacao, which was the name we knew it by when I was posted there. I was told that they did not have a property by that name nevertheless I was welcome to visit Estrela and Lageada. The company did have a third fazenda in those days, called Mutum but I was told that it had been sold already.

Rod Paxton had a few things to buy from the supermarket before heading back to the farm.

"You mentioned that you were on a fazenda called Ligacao," he said as we drove through the very modern Campo Grande, a quantum leap from the scruffy little town I remembered.

"Yes, that was the closest to Campo Grande. Has it been sold?"

"I think you must be thinking of Estrela, which is where we are going. There is an old railway station close by called Ligacao and one of the divisions of the farm in named Ligacao."

"That must be it,' I said." When I was there it was just known as Ligacao."

I was delighted to find that I would indeed be staying at the fazenda where I had been posted all those years ago.

"I have a friend staying with me at the moment, who you may be interested to meet." Rod mentioned, as we were leaving Campo Grande on a wide, open, paved highway. "Richard Turnley used to work for the company until he retired a few years ago. His last post was manager of Tres Barros, where I understand you were stationed."

"Yes, that was my first posting." Things were getting better all the time. Although I would not be visiting Tres Barros, I would be able to compare notes with a man who knew it intimately.

"I was sorry to hear that Tres Barros was changed into a cane sugar estate."

"Well Richard can tell you all about that. He used to manage one of the cattle farms before going to Tres Barros and was given the job of converting it to sugar."

"That must have been hard." I said.

"He was a little uncertain but became very interested in the whole process. You can ask him about it yourself."

My mind went back to my initiation into Brazilian life. I had arrived on a company ship, fresh from England, equipped with a middle class upbringing, a public school education and two years National Service in the British army, stationed in the British Crown Colony of Hong Kong. It would seem to be an unlikely qualification for a Spartan life on the open ranges in the rugged interior of Brazil.

2

THE UNION COLD STORAGE COMPANY

London in November is a great advertisement for the tropics, especially when that is where you have just come from. It was 1956 and I had just completed my two years of compulsory military National Service with the Royal Artillery. My service career had been singularly uneventful, at least from a military standpoint. No medals, no battle scars, not even mentioned in despatches. I had entered the army as 23044592 Gunner Vaughan and two years later I had been demobbed as 23044592 Gunner Vaughan. The bulk of my service, after the initial training in England, had been spent very enjoyably in Hong Kong.

Hong Kong in the early-fifties was a fascinating and exciting place—it was the exotic orient in every sense, yet living in symbiosis with British colonialism. Although the main business centre had a few high rise modern buildings, the majority of the city was still made up of traditional, four to six storey old style Chinese, shops, office and residences. Hong Kong, although recovering from the ravages of war and the years of Japanese occupation, was beginning to feel the economic and social impact of the constant flood of political as well as economic refugees that were pouring daily over the border from the mainland.

Desperate people were fleeing from the effects of civil war and the bite of communism. Some were merchants, professionals or intellectuals fleeing from persecution, others were peasants or workers seeking a better opportunity. The streets were cluttered with beggars, hawkers and street sleepers. Those lucky people who did have jobs, were prepared to work from morning till night, with little chance of holidays, sleeping where they could, often on mats on the factory or shop floor. By contrast the expatriate, mainly British, community lived in a lofty, pampered seclusion on the heights of the Peak; venturing down into the sea level heat only to go to their offices, or on weekends to their golf and country clubs or launches.

I was privileged to be party to several aspects of Hong Kong life. My father was working there at that time, which was why I had given the British Crown Colony as my first choice for posting. My father always claimed that a word in the brigadier's ear had clinched my Hong Kong posting.

It was not unusual for me to take off my gunner's tropical greens, put on a clean set of white shorts—shorts were part of the accepted dress in Colonial Hong Kong in those days—and shirt, and head my 250cc Royal Enfield motor bike over to the Royal Hong Kong Golf Club at Fanling, or the Country Club at Shek O. There I would join my father and the senior members of the British community. The soon to be familiar faces would include doctors, lawyers, judges, with the occasional colonel or even brigadier, with whom my father enjoyed a round of golf amidst the lush unspoilt greenery of the tropical countryside.

The parts of Hong Kong that I loved most were the small, essentially Chinese villages that I visited on my rather battered Royal Enfield. Painting is a hobby that I enjoy and I would spend many a weekend in a traditional little village, somewhere deep in the New Territories. Painting is a great bridge across cultural or language barriers. I found that setting up my easel in a seemingly deserted village worked the same magic as the Pied Piper of Hamlyn. Children, as well as old people, would appear cautiously from the houses, and then with increasing boldness and unrestrained friendliness, gather around me and experience the painting with me. The same would happen in the town, when I sat with sketchpad on my lap. The looks of suspicion, bordering on hostility, that normally greeted a stranger, especially a gwailo, foreign devil, would vanish and laughter would replace them, as they recognized the houses or characters I was portraying.

It had been a great wrench for me, when the time came to be packed, once more, into the P&O troop ship Empress Orwell, for the long, although not uninteresting sea journey back to England. Once there brought back to earth by the grey English weather and the total impersonality of The Royal Artillery's Regimental Headquarters at Woolwich, where I served out my few remaining weeks before being demobbed.

I soon started the job of looking for a career that would take me back to the orient. I had interview after interview but in all cases I would have had to join a firm in England, spend perhaps two to three years, and then, maybe, go overseas. The thought of two or three years of commuting to and working in a grey English city, with equally grey people, was too hard to take. Finally I found a company who wanted people for their farms in Brazil. No farming experience required, training to take place in Brazil. I had spent three summer holidays in Brazil when my stepfather and mother were stationed there, with BOAC (British Overseas Airways Corporation, now British Airways). I set out for the interview with renewed eagerness.

The Vestey's office was housed in an old Dickinsonesque building overlooking the Smithfield Market. I made several passes before finding the small brass plaque that almost apologetically announced the whereabouts of the Union Cold Storage Ltd, the parent company and hub of the Vesteys' vast Empire. The entrance to the building was a far cry from my preconceived ideas of a marble and brass lobby guarding the conglomerate headquarters.

After a preliminary interview by the personnel manager, I was to be interviewed by Mr. Ronald Vestey himself, the multi-millionaire and controlling member of the Vestey family, the huge meat and shipping conglomerate, on whose Empire the sun never set.

"Mr. Vestey is ready to see you now." Mr. Barton, the personnel manager, announced after we had been talking for a few minutes. He led me along a narrow creaking passageway, barely lit by low amperage naked bulbs, which only accentuated the poor state of the paintwork.

"This way." He showed me into a small office, shared by two people. One of the occupants of the office was on the only phone, which was housed in a small telephone booth in one corner of the room. The other occupant, a little old man with a hearing aid, sat at an unimposing, seriously cluttered desk. Mr. Barton withdrew without saying a word, leaving me standing, rather awkwardly, not knowing who I was supposed to talk to.

"You must be young Vaughan," said the man behind the desk, as he indicated a chair opposite, with no more than a cursory glance in my direction. This could not be the millionaire, I thought, it must be the chief clerk, or some assistant getting a few details before ushering me into the big man's office. I sat relaxed talking to this funny little man, who kept asking some rather personal questions but I humoured him.

Mr. Barton re-appeared after a few minutes and escorted me out. Now, I thought, I get to meet the boss. Instead of leading me to the huge carpeted office, with panelled walls and ancestral paintings that I had imagined, Mr. Barton took me back to his own office.

"When do I see Mr. Vestey?" I naively enquired.

"You have just been talking to him," was the surprised and stunning reply.

I had anticipated the usual interview with an inconclusive, 'don't call us we'll call you,' outcome, followed by the long wait for news. I was delighted to find that it was already assumed that I was on my way and all that was needed was to fix the date and settle the terms.

"We are going to give you fifty pounds for clothing," announced Mr. Barton. "I suggest that you buy a good stock of shorts…" I had been in Brazil long enough before to know that, unlike Hong Kong, no one, over the age of five, wore shorts. I smiled and let the remainder of the suggestions wash over me. The upstart of it all was that I would be leaving Birkenhead on MV Debrett, one of their Lamport and Holt ships, on January 3rd 1957. The Vesteys also owned the Blue Star Line, Frederick Layland and Co and the Booth Line, but I knew none of this when I left Smithfield on that cold November morning.

MV Debrett in the British Channel.

3

BOUND FOR RIO

There has been a recurring nightmare in my life of being locked in lavatories. It has happened too many times to be coincidental. I am convinced that there is a conspiracy. The earliest lock-in that I can remember was in Havana, Cuba, when I was visiting my mother and stepfather at the age of twelve. We had been getting ready to go out; I forget where we were going, as we never got there but it must have been somewhere I really wanted to be. I had popped in for a quickie before leaving and there I remained; the door firmly wedged. My mother and I tried all things to open that door but it was not going to budge. I clearly remember at least one meal being passed over the door, where there were some narrow louvers. From time to time my mother came and sat by the door to keep me company, whilst we waited for someone to come.

We were aliens in a foreign land, and their language was not ours. In desperation my mother called the airport, where my stepfather was attending to the weekly BSAA (British South American Airways, later to be taken over by BOAC, then BA) flight from London. He was able to enlist the aid of the airline's airport engineer but only after the flight had taken off, and then a further half an hour for him to drive from the airport.

Eleven years later and thousands of miles away the conspirators struck again. The scene was a small Lamport and Holt cargo ship tied along side a Birkenhead dock, ready to set sail for South America. My Aunt and Uncle, on my father's side, who lived in nearby Wallasey, were on board to see me off. We had spent an hour together, inspecting my cabin, meeting the other passengers, and then going through the repartee of farewell jokes and nuggets of useless advice. My Uncle had worked his way through the imported beers, and my Aunt's constant cycle of small talk was coming round for the third time. Finally there came the welcome call of "all ashore what's going ashore," giving me the chance I had been waiting for to ease springs, whilst my guests made their way down to the dockside.

"I'll be on the boat deck to wave goodbye." I had promised.

I have often wondered what the family was thinking as the ship edged away, taking their young nephew off to his new and exciting adventure. It should have been that poignant moment when streamers cross the widening gap, while a Welsh male voice choir sings Auld Lang Syne, handkerchiefs waving and eyes welling with tears. There was in fact no male voice choir and no streamers. It was only Auntie Kathe and Uncle Jim standing on the quay in the usual Merseyside rain, waiting to wave to their nephew, who was nowhere to be seen. I was, as you may have guessed, incarcerated in a steel tomb with no portholes, deep in the orlop of the ship. The lights of Liverpool to starboard, and those of New Brighton to the port, were but a glimmer in the distance, when I was finally released from my jail. I had been banging and shouting for what seemed like hours, before a passing steward heard my cries and set me free.

Life on board the Lamport and Holt freighter Debrett settled down to normal, punctuated regularly by meals, siestas and sessions at the bar. As the degrees of latitude slipped past the keel, the grey skies and cold winds made way for clear blue skies and that, oh so welcome sunshine. My five fellow passengers were a pleasant enough group. There was a wealthy Anglo-Argentinian Jew from Buenos Aires with his wife and daughter—an attractive girl of seventeen. There was also an elderly couple on their first trip out of England, off to visit their son in Sao Paulo.

The long haul across the South Atlantic was blessed with fairly calm weather and clear skies. I knew I was really on my way, when the crew changed to tropical whites; the signal that England and the winter were really behind us. The change over should have been a day or two earlier but the captain secretly, although everyone knew, spent two days getting his knees brown before having to appear in shorts.

I was on deck early on the morning we arrived in Rio de Janeiro (River of January, named by Portuguese navigators in January 1502). I watched as the familiar peaks of the Rio coastline loomed up on the horizon. I was able, a little later, to make out Copacabana and Leme beaches, with Ipanema and Leblon stretching over the horizon beyond. As the beaches disappeared behind Leme Hill, we entered the narrow channel leading to the harbour. It has been said that the Rio

Harbour is one of the most beautiful harbours in the world. On that day there was nothing to beat it. The entrance to the harbour is dominated by the dramatic rock formations of the Sugar Loaf Mountain in the foreground providing a stunning centrepiece. Beyond and high above the city, the benevolent and beloved statue of the Christo, looked down from his vantage point on top of the high mountain peak, Corcovado.

As we passed along the waterfront of Guanabara Bay, I was able to identify the various bays, with their avenues of trees and wide boulevards. Rio, in those days, could boast some of the world's most dramatic architecture. Its tall buildings, that bordered the long waterfront, were equal to any in the world but they were all put into proper perspective by the sheer magnitude of the dramatic peaks rising above the city and around the harbour.

4

DISCOVERING SAO PAULO

After a 5,750-mile medicinal cruise, a short flight from Rio to Sao Paulo, and a night in the nearest thing to a luxury hotel that I had ever stayed in, I was finally about to meet my employers. Although I had been interviewed in London, I was under contract to the Companhia Frigorifico Anglo or just 'Anglo' as it was generally known. The head office was situated near my hotel; it occupied four floors of a medium size office building.

Anglo was involved in many things. The longer I worked for them, the more surprises I had. All I knew when I walked through the door was that they were involved in cattle farms. My education and introduction into the life of a member of the cattle division started immediately. My first appointment was with the personnel manager, who informed me that I was to be posted to Tres Barros, a citrus and dairy as well as fattening fazenda (farm in the local vernacular) up country in the State of Sao Paulo. During the course of the morning, I was passed from person to person. The Accountant, a rather pompous little man, about as wide as he was tall, his baldness supposedly hidden by a few strands of hair plastered across his head, spent most of the interview lecturing me on VD. It was a subject he seemed to take a delight in, describing the signs and symptoms in graphic detail. The Farms Manager, Roddy Taylor, was very patient with me. He was faced with his latest acquisition, and was clearly not impressed. The recruiting ad had said 'no experience necessary' and I certainly fit the bill. I would get to know and like Roddy later but that first meeting was a little daunting. The climax of my morning came when I was ushered into the office of Peter Allan, the General Manager. He occupied an imposing room that was a lot closer to the image I had had of the millionaire's office, whilst waiting in London to meet Mr. Vestey. Three minutes later I was back in the personnel manager's office, being told that I would leave by train for Pitangueiras, the nearest town to Tres Barros, the following evening. My baggage was due to arrive by truck the following morning from Rio, and then I would be on my way. I was booked into a sleeper car for the over-night trip.

Before being packed off to Pitangueiras, I still had a day and a half to discover Sao Paulo. I was once more on my own and the language barrier was never so high. I was surprised how few people spoke English but then why should they speak my language, I was in their country, I was the foreigner and I realized then that my most important task, in the immediate future, would be to learn Portuguese.

I ventured into a small restaurant for lunch. The menu was of course in Portuguese, and I could not recognize a thing. Many Portuguese words do have some semblance to English but this menu was the exception. The waiter hovered over me, pencil in hand, slight hint of a welcoming smile in the mouth although the eyes and body language said, "Get on with it." In desperation I pointed to two dishes, one I hoped was a soup and the other a main dish. I was of course wrong on both counts. One seemed to be an unrecognisable hors-d'oeuvre and the other must have been a dessert, it was sickly sweet and very glutinous and sat extremely heavily on the stomach. I was no wiser as to what they were, even after tasting and somewhat reluctantly consuming them.

After lunch I went out into the city and walked the streets, just following my nose and exploring. I found a city as modern as any in the world, and yet populated by people who would seem more at home in a small country town, with old customs and beliefs. The atmosphere, off the main thoroughfare where older buildings prevailed, was the same as I would later experience in the small towns in the interior. The street was the market place, the meeting place and the extension of the home. Evenings were spent sitting along the sidewalks, fans in hand, swapping the gossip of the day and calling out to friends passing by. The cooler evening air brought a welcome relief to the day's heat and the stuffiness of small, cramped apartments that many of them lived in. The backdrop to this folksy, rustic scene was a skyline that could hold its own against New York or Chicago.

The following morning, after receiving my baggage, I boarded a *lotacao* on the Avenida Anhangabau, the main thoroughfare in front of my hotel, the Hotel Sao Paulo. A *lotacao* is a small, colourful and often rattly bus that keeps to a route but has no defined stops. If you wanted to board one, you just waved it down, and if you wanted to get off you just told the driver. Various *lotacaos* took me a criss-cross route through Sao Paulo and finally returning me to the Avenida Anhangabau and the hotel.

The streets of Sao Paulo seemed to echo with the sound of sirens, as one passed another approached. I thought that there must be a lot of people in distress, or important people with urgent business. I later discovered that sirens were one of the little perks that any small time official or even non-official was given in return for favours, usually in connection with elections. A later governor of the State of Sao Paulo, Cavalho Pinto was able to do away with these perks and the city became a lot quieter.

My fascinating day of discovery ended in the hotel lobby where I was to meet the accountant, who had been delegated the job of getting me to the station and on to the train. The short drive to the station gave my companion a final chance to fill me with dread and fear of sexual activity. Having spent two years in the British Army I felt sufficiently prepared for the sins of the flesh.

5

STEPPING INTO THE PAST, I GET A HORSE

After a night of rattling across the State of Sao Paulo, the train finally pulled up at a small station that displayed the name that I had been looking for 'PITANGUEIRAS'. The station seemed to be no more than an extension of the street, with the platform barely raised above the street level. I had seen scenes like this in countless westerns, sitting excitedly in the matinee front stalls on cold grey English Saturdays. I expected Gene Autry or John Wayne to come riding up, instead I had to make do with a short, balding but well tanned Frenchman who came forward, shook my hand, grabbed my bags and walked off towards the street. I had to walk at a fair pace to keep up with the man, who turned out to be my immediate boss Bernard Dupont, or 'DP', as he was generally known. DP was in charge of the cattle division of Tres Barros, Vestey's showpiece in Brazil.

Once out of the station, we clambered aboard a rather battered Ford pickup, known as a camionette. Without a word having passed between us, DP jammed the motor into gear, as if he hated the thing, and headed out through the town.

My first rather brief glimpse of Pitangueiras, revealed a small town, with one main square, where most of the more respectable establishments were to be found. The square contained a small park, one side of which was entirely occupied by a huge Roman Catholic Church, by far the largest building in Pitangueiras. Once we had passed through the square, the remainder of the town became steadily more squalid as the paved road gave way to an earth road, long before we had left the town limits.

There were a few vehicles, some camionettes like ours but mostly horse drawn carts and buggies, with a good number of men on horseback. It was still early in the morning to my thinking, being about seven-o-clock, but there was plenty of movement in town. Life in the interior of Brazil, I was soon to find out, starts with the dawn.

We continued on a dusty road leading out of town, passing as we went a few scattered, makeshift houses in smallholdings, where some miserably thin cattle could be seen. Some of the holdings had corn or mandioca growing, and chickens and perhaps a pig, running wild around the yard. We passed some small children, neatly dressed in blue and white school uniforms, walking along the side of the road, trying desperately to avoid our dust. This would become a familiar sight in the years to come. In the more isolated places, children would have to walk miles each day, heading for a small, often one-room school. These children would leave their homes early in the morning and sometimes return home well into the evening, still being expected to do their share of the chores and then their homework, by the light of a candle or spirit lamp.

The boundary of Fazenda Tres Barros was only a few miles from town. It was one of the few fazendas belonging to the company that was so well placed. It did therefore have some social life, partly because of its proximity to town, and also because being a fruit as well as a cattle farm, there were several expatriates stationed there. The citrus divisions were quite concentrated and labour intensive, so required more administration. As we entered the company's land the road improved noticeably. We drove for the first mile or two, through an avenue of orange trees. Occasionally we passed a group of pickers, harvesting the ripe oranges and loading them onto lorries, to be taken to the factory in Pitangueiras. There they went through sorting, dyeing and packing, destined for the fruit shops of Europe. All this I was to learn later, not from my still silent companion.

We left the orange trees behind and came instead into lush pastureland, where I was able to glimpse for the first time, the cattle that would become my life. Occasionally we would pass small clusters of houses, where the farm workers and their families lived; generally far better than the houses I had seen on the road from Pitangueiras. Here too there was usually some mandioca or corn growing, and the inevitable chickens that scattered before us as we drove through.

DP had said almost nothing as we drove from town, which, at the time I mistook for either a bad disposition or bad manners. As I got to know him in the months to come, I realized that he was essentially a shy man, who preferred to say nothing rather than say the wrong thing.

We drew up in front of a white picket fence, beyond which I could see the house that was to be my home, at least a part of it. I was to share the bachelor's quarters with DP and Frank Finch, the only citrus bachelor. The garden was at least an acre, mostly lawn, which was well kept but very bare, devoid of flowers, except for a few bougainvillaea: it was however, amply supplied with mature shade trees, with one tall eucalyptus standing in one corner. There was one other similar house next door; otherwise the garden was surrounded by pasture. A small clutter of workers house could just be seen through some trees further along the mud road in front of the garden. The rather aged wooden bungalow was, like the garden, lacking in both decoration and imagination. It was clean, Spartan but comfortable enough. It was a typical bachelor dwelling that lacked even the slightest hint of the woman's touch.

Frank met us as we reached the veranda steps. He was a tall, fair-haired, cheerful fellow from Cornwell, who gave me a welcoming smile as he reached out and shook my hand warmly. "You must be hungry after that ghastly train journey," he swung the door open and ushered me in. "Breakfast will be ready in a moment."

Frank soon had me feeling as if I belonged. After a quick wash I joined my two companions at the breakfast table. It was hardly the sort of breakfast that I was accustomed to but I was ready to get used to it without any trouble. The steaks were the biggest I had ever seen. To be honest, I had not seen many steaks in my rather sheltered youth. These were larger than the plates, and the plates weren't exactly small. Two eggs, lightly fried, straddled the steaks. There was a pile of toast and a huge pitcher of fresh creamy milk as well as equally fresh orange juice, all, I was told proudly, off the farm.

After another ten-minute drive, the camionette, with the ever-silent DP at the wheel, turned in to the driveway, flanked by towering Royal Palms that had looked down in disdain at the puny endeavours of man, for decades. At the entrance to the drive, the wheels beat a tattoo as they crossed a mata burro (literally 'steer-killer'), a timber grid placed over a deep hole. They are put where a gate would normally be. It stopped the cattle crossing but left the entrance clear for a vehicle to pass through. The mata burros were tremendous time savers. An archway, formed by the stable roof, which connected the adjoining buildings across the road, led us into the sede square.

It was as if I had been transported in a time machine. A scene greeted me that must have remained essentially the same for hundreds of years. Men who would have done Hollywood proud, with wide brimmed hats, long leather boots and spurs, that jangled as they walked, were gathered for the day's orders. Their horses were equally splendid with a variety of saddles and harnesses, decorated with spangles, sheepskins and the essential long whips and coiled lassos, hanging from the saddles. Other men dressed more simply, were feeding calves, or cleaning out the milking shed. A young boy, with a large hat, baggy trousers and bare feet, was heaving a sack of feed into a small buggy, whose scraggy old horse twitched away the flies with his tail.

The sede (the farm centre) was a picturesque cluster of whitewashed farm buildings set around a square open space. It was flanked on one side by the manager's house, set in a large immaculate garden, with fiery Flame of the Forest trees and a row of tall, majestic Pines interspersed with well stocked and lovingly cared-for flower beds. The vibrant colours were dancing in the Brazilian heat, striking a contrast with the three acres of immaculate, lush, green lawn. The remaining three sides of the square contained stables, a granary and the cowshed, flanked by corrals. Perched high on a pole was a dovery, with a few of the white birds basking themselves in the sunlight, whilst others took to the air, as the sound of the twentieth century interrupted their peace. In a corner, beside the old wooden granary, that I later learned had originally housed the slaves, a huge water wheel squeaked and groaned, as a small stream flowed past, added that final touch to the living picture. Was this real? Or had we stumbled into a film set?

I was introduced to the manager Mr. Brown, a tall, slightly stooped Welshman in his late fifties, who greeted me in a rather peremptory manner as if he had a lot on his mind. As I got to know him I realized that he always seemed to be a little preoccupied in a rather vague, far away manner. His wife, his total opposite, appeared momentarily to offer me an enthusiastic welcome.

"Have you done any farming before?" asked Mr. Brown, after we had exchanged the barest of pleasantries.

"I spent some time on a farm as a child." I offered.

"Can you ride?" I had done a little pony riding, so I volunteered the information. DP and Mr. Brown exchanged glances.

"Well, the next few months will make a rider out of you, and maybe even a farmer." Put in DP, in one of his most vocal outbursts so far.

With my credentials presented, we went back to the sede square, where an unexpected number of people seemed to be assembled. When we had arrived earlier I was the spectator, now, it appeared, I was the spectacle, the new '*Ingles*' greenhorn.

"This is Zeze," DP explained, indicating a young man with a black wide brimmed hat, who gave me a bright, almost boyish smile as he shook my hand. "You will be working with him between milkings. I'll take you to the retiro, where you will be milking, later." With that he turned and went back to the office, or so I thought.

I followed Zeze to the corral, where he chose a horse for me. To my relief, he chose a quiet, mature, working horse called Pitangueiras, named after the local town. Pitangueiras was saddled for me and led out into the square. We were, it appeared, ready to go. I was helped into the Brazilian saddle, which was a simplified version of the American saddle, the main difference being that there was only a slight forward raise of the front of the saddle, with no rounded pommel. The stirrups were altered to suit my legs although they were set a lot longer than I was expecting. I slowly became aware that the crowd was still very interested, and seemed to be waiting for something. Zeze handed me the reins and stood back. I looked around, waiting for the others to mount.

As my eyes swept the scene, I became aware of three faces that should not have been there. DP was hovering just near the office door. Mr. Brown was apparently inspecting the rear tyre of DP's camionette and the diminutive Mrs. Brown, who I had just met briefly, was rather nervously clutching the banister of the kitchen steps. A bell rang in my head, but too late. There was a movement behind me, and my quiet, docile, animal suddenly became a wild, demented, beast, leaping, snorting and twisting. He then headed for the exit and the open field beyond. Pitangueiras was like one possessed, head down, ears pressed to his head, kicking his hind legs as he went. I had instinctively grabbed the saddle and continued to hold on out of shear terror. My legs had parted company with the stirrups and were waving around like so much seaweed on a stormy coast. A wild kaleidoscope of black and white buildings, mixed with green trees and blue sky, began to meld together. I was about finished, my arms could not hold any more. Hands suddenly grabbed me and mercifully lowered me to the ground. It was Zeze and one of his men.

As I sat there wide-eyed, shaking like a fat lady on a runaway cart I was congratulated by a mob of smiling faces. Hands reached down to pat me on the back and help me to my feet. I found out later what it was that had turned my quiet friendly horse, into a mad demon. One of the cowboys had lifted Pitangueiras's tail and put a thorny branch where it would make itself felt. The poor horse could not win; the more he jumped the more it hurt. The Brazilian cowboy loves a joke, and a greenhorn Ingles, fresh off the ship was fair game.

My initiation was over, and my exciting and fascinating association with the Brazil and the Brazilian cowboys had begun.

Zeze

6

A MOST UNLIKELY COWBOY

For my first three months as a Brazilian cowboy, I was under Zeze's command for the middle part of the day. Early each morning, and again in the evening, I went to one of the milking retiros, to help with the milking. I woke each day at five in the morning, went out to the paddock near the house to find and saddle my horse Pitangueiras, and then rode him to the retiro. It would still be quite dark at that time of the morning and surprisingly cold, as we rode out to the field to round up the cows. Most of the cows would be waiting at the gate, so it was usually no great problem. There was however often one who just wanted to be different, or was sick or lame and we had to set out to find her.

The cows would start calling their calves as we approached the milking corral, and the calves answered with the desperate cries of hungry children. There were no separate stalls for the cows as one would find in an English farmyard. Milking was done out in the open corral. Calves were let out one by one and allowed to suckle from their mothers for a few moments, just long enough to get the milk to run. Then they were tied, protesting loudly, to the mother's foreleg. A rope secured the cow's hind legs, so that she could not walk away.

The vaceiro (cowman) squatted down on a little one-legged stool, to milk the cow. Learning to milk a cow was quite easy, although learning to control the one legged stool was quite a different matter. A thin leather strap around the waist secured the stool. It had to be just loose enough, so that as the milker squats down, the single leg drops to the perpendicular and so takes the weight; that is at least the theory. Many were the times when the theory, as well as my stool, let me down. Being let down by a one-legged stool in a freshly manured milking corral can have disastrous results, not only to my fragile ego but also to my body odour and social graces.

The cold of the early morning slowly turned to warmth, and then, all too soon, to blistering heat, as the day progressed. The tangled knot in my stomach began to remind me that I was hungry. We always left one of the cows, whenever possible the one with the creamiest milk, for the last. A rather battered mug was produced, and we took our turn to pump the rich, warm milk onto a mixture of Toddy (a chocolate powder. Not the lethal coconut wine of the same name that stupefies the Tamil labour force, on the rubber plantations in Malaya) sweetened with a good dose of the fine powdery Brazilian sugar, to make a rich warm drink that was one of the highlights of the day.

The morning's milking over and the calves fed, their mothers were returned to the field, to make some more revenue producing milk. I mounted my horse and headed home for that breakfast of kings, a large steak and eggs, to which I was becoming well accustomed. There was little time to relax however; Zeze and the commitiva would be waiting for me for a day's work in the pastures.

The commitiva was made up of most of the vaceiros who were not needed on the retiro between milking. Usually the retireiro, the man in charge of the retiro (division) would keep one assistant, for the routine work and lend the remainder to Zeze for the commitiva.

Each day seemed to present a new, fascinating and often exciting experience, especially for a young guy fresh out from England. We would be branding one day, vaccinating another, perhaps castrating, counting or culling, on another. There was one thing that most days had in common and that was the moving of cattle. We had to bring them to the corral, round them up for counting, or just change their pasture. Besides the dairy herd, we also had a good number of steers for fattening. Many of the steers were our own castrated male calves but also some came from other farms in Mato Grosso do Sul, or bought by the company's cattle buyer in the Pantanal and sent to us by train for fattening. I would get to know that end of things later. The fattening steers were kept in the furthest pastures and so there was a good deal of cattle moving to be done.

The herding of cattle is done quietly and gently. There is very little of the yelling and whip cracking, as seen on the movies. Milk cows can stop producing milk if they are badly frightened, and steers can lose weight. The exception to the gently-gently manoeuvre was when we were taking a bunch of newly weaned calves out to pasture on that first fateful day away from mum. The youngsters had but one thing on their minds, and that was to get back close to their mothers. There was no herd instinct amongst these young animals; they were just a group of determined individuals looking out for number one. It took the whole commitiva, plus a lot of shouting and whip cracking, to persuade these young rebels to leave their mothers and start a new life.

After a few weeks I was beginning to find my seat on horseback, chasing after cattle like the best of them. I must be honest and give my horses credit, they knew more about rounding up cattle than I would ever know. Once I indicated to my horse that I wanted to go after a runaway, my only responsibility then, was to stay in the saddle. Because I was on horseback every day I had acquired two more horses, so that I could rotate them.

My first real dash after a steer ended in disaster. A steer had broken from the herd and, finding that he was alone, had panicked. He put his head down and ran, paralleling the fence. I happened to be closest and, seeing my chance to play the cowboy, spurred my horse and we shot off after the steer. I was still riding like an English squire, gripping with the knees, weight well forward. We bore down on the steer, cutting in at an angle to the fence. The steer saw us and stopped, turned, and headed off in the opposite direction. My horse also stopped, turned, and headed off in the opposite direction in hot pursuit. I however continued on, with my knees bent and my elbows held close to my body, in the direction we had been heading. I suffered no serious injury except a further jolt to my already fractured ego.

After a few weeks with the team I was beginning to understand a little Portuguese, mainly by the monkey-hear-monkey-say method. I used to make some terrible mistakes and the men would laugh and pull my leg, though they always put me right. Zeze was a great teacher; he would point things out as we rode and pronounce the word several times and then get me to say it. Any slight mistake was greeted by laughter from the team but the right pronunciation was rewarded by applause. There were several expressions that I picked up from the Brazilians which were, to say the least, rather colourful. I found out just how colourful when in all innocence I let one out in female company and was met with a stony, embarrassed silence from the women and stifled laughter from the men.

Slowly I was becoming less of a liability and was even able to take the place of one of the men on a trail, or lend a hand during branding or vaccinating. I was determined to become skilled with the lasso and I spent hours practising, often secretly in the garden. After we had finished the milking, I lassoed the bigger calves that refused to return to their pen. Lassoing in the corral is nearly always done on foot. First you get the calves to move round the corral, picking out the one you want to catch. Standing near the middle of the corral, you start swinging a large loop of the lasso, with one or two smaller loops held in the same hand. As the long loop swings over your head you lock your eyes onto the victim. When he is in range and the lasso is swinging at the right speed, you let it go on the up swing so that the loop, diminishing as it flies away, forms a snare just in front of the calf or steer, so that it literally runs into the noose. It then takes a quick jerk of the hand to tighten the lasso.

Setting the loop over the head is only a part of the problem. Having done it you are now attached to a very strong and frightened young animal that can pull the lasso right out of your hands. The art of controlling the snared beast is to throw the weight of the body behind the foot furthest from the animal, just as the tension is taken on the lasso. The rawhide lasso is draped over the thighs, with the rear hand pushing down hard, with the other hand guiding the direction of the pull. For a while you do a little crab dance, being pulled forward, and then jumping backward, until you get the lasso round the tethering pole, that is present in any corral. With a quick loop round the pole you have the quarry where you want him. It all sounds quite straightforward but when you have a few hundred pounds of frightened muscle at the end of your lasso, a slight miscalculation can leave you flat on your face, and if you forget to let go, you can be dragged around the corral like an extra tail.

I became pretty cocky with the young calves but graduating to a full-grown steer, first in the corral and then on horseback, was not achieved without considerable bruising, blistering and a lot of laughter, always at my expense but good natured.

My graduation came quite by accident. I was in the right place at the right time. It could easily have proven to be the wrong place and the wrong time. Several of the steers had broken away and scattered. With no more than a nudge from me Pitangueiras and I joined in the chase. I felt the full power of the magnificent animal as my calm gentle horse surged forward like a racehorse coming out of the gate and powered across the terrain. Almost immediately I found myself within range of one of the runaway steers, with my lasso swinging, eager to prove itself. With all the skill I could muster I released the loop and watched with sheer delight, as the noose fell neatly over the steer's horns. With a flick of the wrist, the noose drew taut and my horse turned to take the strain.

I turned to see who had witnessed my prowess but to my horror there wasn't a soul in sight. Now I had seen all this before and had even helped to throw a steer or two, with one man on the tail and the other turning the head causing the animal to fall. The old hands do it alone, with the horse taking the strain on the lasso. I had no illusions as to being an old hand nevertheless here I was with a horse at one end of my lasso and a very unhappy, full grown steer at the other. I was definitely out-numbered.

Well there is no heroic outcome to this little anecdote; it was definitely a stalemate. The commitiva found me after a while and to the accompaniment of a chorus of good-natured banter and laughter, the odds returned to normal. The important thing was that I had taken the challenge to put what I had learned into practice and, as an experienced pilot will tell you, 'any landing that you can walk away from, is a good landing.' I had walked away from that one, and, to my credit, the steer had been caught. In the months to come I had many such encounters and I gradually earned my spurs. I did not actually use spurs; I always felt that they were unnecessary and cruel.

Pedro, one of the cowboys, suddenly waved us to a halt and signalled for silence. I looked around for the cause of his sudden action, but noticed nothing unusual. We were returning from one of the paddocks after returning some cattle. Before I had any idea what was happening, Pedro leapt from his horse and dived into a small pond close to the path, it was only then that I noticed a snake's head, barely breaking the surface of a small pond. Pedro had grabbed the snake's neck just behind the head. I am sure that the snake was surprised but not nearly so much as the Pedro was. What had at first sight, appeared to be a relatively small Anaconda, turned out to be a massive snake. The entire pool came alive with coils. Soon this huge snake was wrapping itself many times round the hapless cowboy. The snake's body was so thick that you could not get two hands around it.

For a moment the other cowboys looked on with humour, however they soon realized that the man was in serious trouble. The anaconda had a very strong grip on him and a large part of the tail was forcing his head back dangerously. All hands took to the water and the cowboys' ever present skinning knives soon had the throat cut. Pedro was badly bruised and severely shaken but had been saved by the fact that there were no trees or roots close by for the Anaconda to use as a leverage. Had the anaconda been able to anchor his tail, the poor man might not have survived. The skin, carefully preserved, became a talking point on the farm; it was a good thirty feet in length. The skin was presented to Mr. Brown, who paid for it to be cured. He would theatrically spread this huge snakeskin down the length of the veranda, to the amazement of his guests.

My first horse, Pitangueiras,

7

A MAKEE-LEARN VET

The first real job I had, after finishing my basic training, came about as a result of one of the earlier breeding experiments, which had been started a few years prior to my arrival. Tres Barros was primarily concerned with milk cattle, and we were trying to find a breed that would survive the hot Brazilian climate. It was important to find or develop a breed to give a better yield of milk than the local breed of Zebu, the Gyr, Guzerat or Nelore Indian humped cattle. The Indian cows gave a very good quality of milk, in terms of butterfat but the quantity was far from economical. Being a long way from the major cities, we were not in the quality dairy milk market. The fazenda was under contract to Catupiri, a cheese manufacturing company that was more interested in quantity than quality.

European dairy cattle had, for many years, been used in the more temperate parts of Brazil and also in places where the price of milk could pay for special treatment for the cows. We had to graze the cattle under normal open country in tropical conditions. The first experiment involved a cross between Friesian bulls and the local Zebu cows. It was hoped that the result would be a sturdy cow that could stand the tropical climate and produce milk in greater quantities than the local cattle. The first cross had been fairly successful, producing a straight fifty-fifty cross but the next step had produced a three quarter Friesian, one quarter Zebu strain, and the young calves were dying like flies. The poor little things did not seem to have any resistance and were prone to anything that was going around.

Unlike an English dairy farm, there were no vets doing house calls. The nearest vet to Tres Barros was in Barretos, four or five hours away by car.

"I've got a job for you," DP announced one morning, with his customary abruptness. "I want you to spend your time doing what you can to keep these calves from dying. We have received a shipment of a variety of medicines from Sao Paulo. Do your best to save these animals."

My veterinary academic training came from reading the labels on the boxes; luckily some of them were in English. The practical training came from trial and error. Hardly the qualifications for a James Herriot but they were the best that we had.

I spent most of my mornings going from retiro to retiro in a little horse and buggy. Armed with boxes of medicines and syringes and a few simple surgical instruments, I went around visiting my patients, like the old time village doctor. My practice gradually extended to the whole farm, as all animals are liable to get sick. From time to time we would spend a weekend of R&R in Barretos, where the company had a meat factory. I was able to use those visits to get a lot of useful advice, by picking the brains of some of the other farm managers as well as the government vet, who was in charge of meat inspection at the factory.

Not only did the good vet give me a good deal of useful advice but also a few more instruments and an old, although still useable, stethoscope. So my medical bag as well as my knowledge increased with each visit. Everybody chipped in to educate the new, makee-learnee vet. I learnt the old method of bleeding from the retireiros, which was especially useful for horses when they became run down. It was quite incredible the difference that it could make. My first introduction to bleeding came when one of horses had become thin and generally run down. There seemed to be nothing particularly wrong, so we left him out in the pasture for two weeks, expecting him to start to recover after a few days. Normally a rest was all that was needed, though in this case there was no improvement.

"I think we should bleed him," decided Raoul, the older of the retireiros, who was also the father, or grandfather of half the commitiva. He returned to the house and fetched his bleeding knife, an instrument that looked like a pocket-knife, except that it had a conical-shaped blade, which protruded at right angles to the shaft for half an inch at the end.

"Hold his head firmly," Raoul ordered his grandson, a sturdy boy of sixteen, who helped in the retiro. "He may jump a little but you must keep him still." He located the main vein of the horse's neck; he then put a rope round and wedged a plug of wood wrapped in a cloth against the vein, pulling the rope tight. The vein bulged. The horse's eyes also bulged with fear as he struggled to breathe.

"Keep him still now." Raoul placed the sharp blade across the bulge, and gave it a sharp tap with a whip handle. The blood gushed out of the wound, flowing into a bucket held for the purpose.

"See how watery the blood is. We must wait until the blood looks thicker before stopping the flow." I watched in horrified fascination as the blood poured into the bucket. The horse held quite still, although his eyes were wide open and staring in obvious fear. The blood was just beginning to look a little thicker, when the horse's legs seemed to buckle. "'That's enough." said Raoul, releasing the rope and pressing his thumb hard against the wound. He held it there for a few moments, and then let go. The bleeding had stopped but the horse, although relieved that he could now breathe without difficulty, was obviously still a little shaky.

Two weeks after the bleeding the horse was looking better than I had ever seen him. The coat had a gloss. He had regained a lot of weight, and a healthy sparkle replaced the dull glassy stare that his eyes had had previously.

I put my heart into learning everything I could about treating sick animals although I was of course shot-gunning most of the time. If there were a fever or any septic sore, I would use penicillin or terramicine. An undernourished and weak calf would get some liver extract under the skin. The worst and most common condition I had to face was diarrhoea, which was hard to fight. The poor bewildered calves were unable to hold any food or even fluid, and could die very quickly. It was heartbreaking to see these young calves suffer, weaken and die in spite of all my efforts. I could not help but become emotionally involved and suffer with them.

I was called whenever there was sickness or injury to any of the cattle. I found that I had to turn my hand to many things. One of the retireiros called me one day because his best cow had been kicked in the udder, and the inflammation had caused one of the teats to become badly inflamed.

"I am afraid this teat has become gangrenous." I said, after looking at the cow. One section of the udder was grossly enlarged and the teat was a dark green. "The only chance we have of saving her is to remove one quarter of the udder, and hope that we can save the others."

The retireiro shook his head. "She is a good cow this one, she has produced some of my best calves. I would hate to lose her."

"I'll get what I need and come back later."

"DP, I've got a very sick cow with a gangrenous teat. I want to try to save it if I can. The only thing I can do is to try to remove a section of that udder."

"If it's gangrenous already, there is not much we can do." DP looked up from his desk, as I stood still panting at the door. "It is better to just put her down than to prolong the suffering, besides you have never done any surgery before. I admire your enthusiasm but that is a bit ambitious."

"I want to give a try," I said. "I had a volunteer job once in a hospital, working in the theatre, and I have watched many operations. In the emergency unit I even helped stitch on a number of occasions. I realize that does not make me a surgeon, nevertheless I want to try to save that cow."

DP looked at me for a moment, then without speaking, headed for the door, indicating that I should follow. As we headed out of the sede, DP turned the camionette towards the town. After a while DP broke the silence.

"If you are going to become a surgeon, we must at least get you some more instruments. I am sure Doc Moreno will lend us some."

Doc Moreno, the farm's GP, did more than that, probably breaking every ethic in the medical book. "So you want to perform a mastectomy do you?" He looked at me in amusement. "Have you decided how to anaesthetize the cow?"

"Not yet." I admitted.

"She's not going to just lie there quietly while you cut off her tit." He dug into the cupboard and came out with a large bottle of ether, some wads of gauge and a number of instruments. "You say you have had some experience with stitching. Well let's go over it a little, the important thing is to tie off bleeders. Small ones you can cauterize, some thin hot irons would serve for that." He gave me a quick rundown of the possible problems I might face.

We thanked both the man and the doctor, who later became a good friend, and set off back to Tres Barros. Armed with my instruments, ether, antibiotics and friendly advice, I headed off for the retiro.

With the help of the retireiro and two of his men, we put the cow down on her side on a part of the floor that had been well hosed.

"Get her tied so that she cannot kick but keep the legs spread, so as to keep the udder well exposed." I ordered. Once the cow was ready, I placed the gauze over her nose and started to drip the ether. After a few anxious moments while we struggled to keep her down, she started to give up the fight and lay still.

I handed over the job of dripping ether on to the gauze to Pedro one of Raoul's many sons and took up my position facing the injured udder.

"Well here goes." I made a few jabs, to make sure that she was feeling no pain, before I started to cut. The blood gushed and I was soon busy clamping the bleeders and mopping the blood.

"Pass me the hot iron.' I ordered. I quickly cauterized the bleeders, before releasing the forceps. I was relieved to see that the bleeding had stopped. "Keep those irons hot, we are going to need them many times before this day is out."

Once I had completely exposed the section of the udder, I had to look for major blood vessels, and, using the catgut, tie them off before removing the breast.

"How is she looking Raoul?"

"She seems to be breathing steadily, Senhor. You're doing OK." He gave me a reassuring tap on the shoulder. Young Pedro nodded his assurance that all was well.

"There are a lot of blood vessels here," I said, as the sweat was beginning to roll into my eyes. "We must make sure they are all secure, or she will bleed to death."

After I had removed the entire breast, I cut away enough skin, so that I could sew her up neatly. I left the last bit of the wound open, just enough to allow for a small rubber drain. "She is going to get some infection after this, so we have to leave that drain for a while, to let the pus out." I explained. "She will be quite a sick cow for a week or so."

"We will take care of her." Raoul assured me.

Pedro showed me the bottle of ether; it was nearly finished. With a smile of relief he lifted off the gauze and allowed the cow to slowly come round. We stayed with her until she was able to regain her feet.

After a few days, and a lot of care from Raoul and the boys, she turned the corner and showed definite signs of recovery. I made several visits to change dressings, which are very hard to keep on a cow's udder, and to administer doses of antibiotic. My star patient pulled through. Her calf had to be weaned early but luckily he was already fairly old. I am glad to be able to relate that to Raoul's and my delight, she had more calves and gave milk from the three remaining teats.

Some of the common problems that I had to face in my veterinary rounds, were the cold cysts that could often be found; they needed to be lanced, to prevent them from bursting on their own, and causing a stream of pus down the fur. The pus would attract the flies, resulting in a wound swarming in maggots. When the cyst is ready, a small thin spot can be palpated in the centre of the bump. With a sharp knife, this area can be lanced and the cyst drained. I must have lanced hundreds of these cysts and it was quite common to get a cup-full of pus out of a small calf. These cysts did not seem to give the animal any pain; in fact I suffered more from looking at them than they seemed to. Some of these cysts were the result of a warble fly larva that had died in the skin, remained inside and had gone bad.

The warble fly was a constant nuisance, and dozens of the larvae could be found in the skin of an animal. They seemed to prefer the animals with dark fur, and the Friesian cross cattle were particularly vulnerable. The older animals were sprayed regularly with an insecticide that killed off the ticks, as well as the warble fly, but the young animals were not sprayed, for safety sake. It was important to try to rid the calves of the warble fly whenever they could be found. As the calves were handled daily, it was not too difficult to have a look at them, while they were being sorted at milking time. They were then taken care of when the cows had been let out after milking.

It was not uncommon to find a cluster of the larvae in the skin. When they were coming to the surface, they could be squeezed out. The white larva would pop to the surface with the slightest squeeze, giving one all the satisfaction of a very ripe boil.

I have only seen the warble fly in a human once. The carpenter somehow got a cluster of three larvae in the armpit, and the poor man suffered terribly before we were able to get them out. Cattle have more mobile skin and so perhaps they don't suffer too much; nevertheless it always distressed me to see the little calves with the wretched things pushing through their skin.

Mastitis was fairly common. I was forever draining thick putrid fluid from a cow's teat. We had ointments to put up into the teat but the draining was most important. I would visit as often as possible to keep the offending teats drained; usually they cleared up quite quickly.

Tres Barros. Looking from the corral towards the old slave house.

8

A DIFFICULT BIRTH

Cows usually need no assistance when giving birth but occasionally there were complications, and some help was needed. After some trial and error I became quite adept at turning a calf in the womb, when the calf was presenting in an awkward position. I spent many a long session with my arm inside a cow's womb, struggling to find a leg or a nostril. Providing the calf came out alive, all the struggling was worth it. There was nothing so depressing as fighting, sometimes in the dead of night, bare belly covered in cow dung, both arms smeared with a mixture of soap and mucus, and dead weary, only to deliver a lifeless form.

Only once did I have to cut a calf out. I had been counting cattle on one of the retiros all that day. Something I had to do every month for stock taking. I had arrived home exhausted, rather late. Somehow things had not gone too well in the counting, we had had to recount on several occasions, and on the last count there was still one missing. The retireiro was certain that they had all been there the previous day, so we had made a fruitless search, only to find that he had made a mistake in his bookkeeping.

DP and Frank had gone into town, so the house was quiet, ideal for the sleep I was looking forward; unfortunately I didn't get very much. I became aware of the sound of some one clapping his hands in front of the house; this was the usual way of attracting attention, rather than knocking on the door. I dragged myself from my bed and peered out of the door.

"Good evening Senhor, my father has sent me to ask you to come to the retiro." It was young Chico from one of the Zebu retiros. This was a fairly familiar event, though not usually from the Zebu herd. It was usually a calf dying or a cow having a difficult birth. I sometimes prided myself that the retireiros called me because of my great knowledge but really they called me so that if anything went wrong, they could pass the blame on to me.

"What is the trouble amigo?" I asked.

"One of the cows, Senhor, she is having trouble dropping her calf."

D.P. had the camionette, so I climbed aboard the boy's horse, and, with him hanging on behind me, rode into the night.

The cow was looking bad when I got there, she had been struggling for some time, and there was no presentation. It was not her first calf, and she was a fair size, so there was no obvious reason except for a breech. I stripped to the waist, washed my arms and started to make my inspection. Somehow the little occupant had got his leg all tied into a knot. The hind leg was tucked up behind the shoulder, and the head was twisted backwards but the most important find was that the little fellow was dead. The body, although warm, was lifeless and inert. Sometimes as I explored, a live calf would nudge me out of the way, or pull back, and some times even suckle at my finger as I found his mouth. This one had given up the struggle before it had begun.

The cow seemed to sense that her calf was dead, as she had lost interest in the proceedings, and seemed too tired and listless to push. I lay spread-eagle on the ground, trying desperately to reposition the calf but somehow there was always something stopping the delivery. The cow was weak and exhausted.

"There is nothing I can do for the calf," I told the retireiro," but we must try to save the cow."

"We have to try to cut the calf out Senhor, she is a good cow, and I don't want to lose her."

I could not get a knife inside without injuring the cow, so I had a brainwave.

"Chico. Would you let me borrow a guitar string?" I had seen the boy playing on his guitar on previous visits.

"Si Senhor." He headed for the house without questioning. He unstrung the first string and I tied a cord to either end. I threaded the cord through the calf's groin and placed a cloth around the entrance to the womb, to avoid cutting the cow. I started sawing with the wire string.

I lay on my side, naked to the waist, sawing and repositioning the calf, until bit by grisly bit, I was able to dismember the poor creature. Resembling a scene from Dante's inferno I kept bringing out my macabre handiwork, like a mad magician, until the last ounce of flesh was excavated, followed by the placenta, and then my gruesome work was done.

I sat exhausted surrounded by carnage, and became aware for the first time that the other cows were in the corral. The early morning milking was just beginning.

One of the unpleasant tasks I had to perform was to try to clean out a cow's uterus when the placenta had remained inside. The result of this can be very serious, as the placenta goes bad quite quickly. Soon the uterus is full of a putrid mass, which has to be removed, and the whole uterus cleaned out. After performing this feat, I was usually covered in pus and decaying matter. I had to head for home for a shower and change of clothing. Even then I found people giving me strange looks, and keeping their distance.

The prolapsed uterus was also fairly common. I would often be presented with the sight of the entire uterus hanging free from the vagina. Sometimes they would stay after being replaced but often I had to stitch the side of the vagina for a few days to hold it in place but even this was not always successful

I was learning a lot by experience but in spite of all that many of the calves died; some I'm sure would have died even under the best care although I am sure that many would have lived, had we had a vet. Every time one of the animals died, the retireiro would ask me why it had died. Sometimes I could give him a satisfactory answer, though often I would have to say, with all the sincerity that I could muster," O coracao paro." (The heart stopped) They seemed to be satisfied with this explanation but I was not. I always wanted to know why, and what more I could have done, or what I had done that I should not have.

We learnt by our mistake with the Friesian cross, and turned our breeding attention to a Red Poll cross, which was eventually a successful new breed of five eighths Red Poll, three eighths Zebu, and is called Pitangueiras. I was able to see some very handsome young bulls before I left, however it took many years to fix the breed.

9

GETTING TO KNOW THE NEIGHBOURS, CARNIVAL

Social life on Tres Barros revolved around a small clubhouse, set on a man-made lake, surrounded by vast areas of citrus trees. The club had a tennis court and a small wooden pier on the lake. We could swim in the lake most of the year; after a long dry spell it became difficult. There was also a small rowing boat if someone wanted to fish or just paddle across the lake. There were four British fruit people on the farm besides Mr. Brown, who was the over all manager, Frank Finch my bachelors' quarters house mate, Ian McCullock and his wife who were our immediate neighbours, David Harrison was there for a short time after I arrived, I did not get to know him very well but liked him. He left Tres Barros believing, due to a little misunderstanding, that he was to take over as manager of Sao Sebastiao, the company's banana estate. I would get to know him better later. John Jarrold replaced David, having just returned from leave with his new bride Chris. The last members of the farm group were Eric Seddon and his wife Maria. Eric had been around for many years and was married to a Brazilian lady and was more Brazilian than the Brazilians. Keith Prowse, the factory manager occasionally came out from the town. He ran the plant where the oranges were washed dyed and packed. Keith's wife had been a fashion model before they married; she still had her looks as well as her figure and somehow seemed out of place in the interior of Brazil, she rarely left Pitangueiras. DP, who was a Brazilian born Frenchman, and I, along with the wives, made a total of twelve people, not a bad little social circle. The Seddons had two sons and a daughter, who spent their school holidays on the farm and helped to liven things up a little.

It was a pleasant break on a Sunday, when we were able to meet other people, play a little tennis, have a swim and sometimes enjoy a barbecue. This clubhouse was also the venue for the company's annual farm's weekend, during which all the farm managers and assistants from around Brazil, as well as some of the brass from Sao Paulo, would gather for a weekend.

One of the strangest characters on Tres Barros was the irrepressible John Jarrold. He had recently returned from leave in England with his new bride Chris. John was as close to a bull in a china shop as one could imagine. He was the sort of person to whom those things that just couldn't really happen in real life, happened frequently. I remember going along for the ride one evening when John and Frank were working late on some new irrigation project. For some reason they were having trouble with a new heavy-duty pump. The motor was working well but nothing was coming out. There was an interesting contrast between the tall, fair, unflappable Frank and the short, stocky totally flappable John, who was racing around in his usual manner, giving orders to all and sundry. After looking at the motor and the various couplings, John finally stood in frustration at the business end of the pipe and looked into it. I can only presume that he wanted to see if the water was coming. Well it just so happened that it was, and it knocked John clear into the main drain, which was already very muddy.

Another time John was standing beside a caterpillar tractor, giving minute-by-minute orders to the driver, who had been doing the job for years. Finally the driver got down in frustration and suggested, very politely, that it would be quicker if John did the job himself, which he promptly tried to do. Within minutes he managed to turn the thing upside down, almost on top of himself.

The Jarrolds were very fond of animals. They had a house and garden full of every type of creature that you could think of, and a few that you wouldn't. One of the most bizarre was a vulture that they had found and rescued as a young chick. They had brought it up from cute chick to ugly adult in their garden. I could never get used to seeing the very English girl-next-door Chris coming along the road to where we killed the weekly cow, with a vulture circling over her head.

Another creature that had a brief stay in their house was a small alligator. The locals sometimes hunted the small alligators that were present in a few of the, quite large, man-made irrigation lakes on the farm. I went out a few times with the men, quite late on moonless nights, cramped together in a small boat just wide enough to sit in. The locals hunted the alligators at night for a good reason; they were armed with a strong torch and a small wire snare on a pole. The torchlight would hypnotize the alligators and cause them to remain motionless in the water. The light would be reflected brightly from the alligator's eyes, like cat's eyes on a dark stretch of road. Once the men in the boat saw the reflection, complete silence was imperative as they paddled quietly towards the reptile. The man holding the light had to keep it very steady, as the boat edged towards the hypnotized alligator. If the light wavered the spell would be broken and the alligator would quickly dive under the water. With skill and considerable experience the hunters could get right alongside the alligator and snare it. John had caught one on one of our hunting trips, and had then felt sorry for it and decided to keep it rather than eat it, as the hunters would have done. He took it home and installed it in splendour in the spare bath. He must have heard about alligators being tamed in circuses, so he tried. His first move was to put his hand down to stroke the reptile. I don't think the alligator got the message at all. He took a chunk out of John's finger and found himself back in the lake.

The owl was rather amusing. He was quite tame and would sit in the room with us, watching with unblinking eyes. One evening when Frank and I were visiting the Jarrolds, we put the owl on a chair in the middle of the room and walked round him. He was able to follow us for one and a quarter turns, before whipping round and continuing to follow us. We stopped after a while for fear of strangling him.

Chris Jarrold was pregnant and becoming more so every day. I don't know whether you have ever seen a pregnant tennis player, playing in the briefest of slips, well into the final stages of pregnancy. It is not a pretty sight and there was no doubt that she was pregnant. Chris was determined to share her pregnancy with all of us. Her conversations usually turned to the subject. She invariably reminded us that she had been a nurse before being bowled off her feet by John and transported to the back of beyond. She had of course seen thousands of deliveries and knew exactly what to expect. She knew all the signs and was not going to panic.

A very elaborate plan evolved to get her to Ribeirao Preto when the time eventually came. The plan involved almost the entire farm, with every sort of fail-safe contingency imaginable. At three o-clock one morning operation 'Chris transport' suddenly became a reality and swung into action. John called Eric, his division manager who dragged himself out of bed and rushed over to pick up the couple. He drove them down to the sede to arouse Nogeiro, the office clerk cum company driver. Eric Seddon then went home. Nogeiro, never a bundle of laughs at the best of time, punctuating his driving with muttering and crashing of gears, drove the couple to the McCullocks' house, our only neighbours. Frank Finch had volunteered to drive the back-up vehicle, so the bachelors' house was also roused. The convoy set off for the three-hour drive to Ribeirao Preto. It was an earth road all the way, which turned to mud with a little rain and of course it rained that night.

Chris had been giving a blow-by-blow account of the pains and their frequency, and was confident that the baby would be ready to appear by the time they arrived at the hospital. Ian, Frank and Nogeiro returned six hours later, after depositing the couple at the hospital. There was no definite news about the delivery from the drivers but we expected to hear something soon. A week went by, and there was still no happy news. Mr. Brown had some business in Ribeirao Preto and went to visit the couple in the hospital. The hospital staff told him that the Jarrolds were out shopping. Mr. Brown went about his business in town, only to bump into the two Jarrolds strolling hand in hand along the main street. Chris was still very pregnant.

I occasionally had to cut through the fruit division on my way from one part of the farm to another. I often stopped and selected a prize orange to quench my thirst. As I reached for a particularly juicy fruit one day a memory flashed through my mind of the first orange I ever remember seeing, not tasting only seeing. My mother had taken a job in a small boarding school for very young children. I do not know the arrangement but my brother and I, being of the right age, were enrolled in the school. It was in the early years of the war and my father had been called up for active service, so my mother had to cope with two small children alone. The headmistress was the typical cold authoritarian figure, so typical of that period. She seemed to hate children and should never have been allowed anywhere near them. One Sunday my mother asked permission to take her two sons out for the day. After some rather heated argument, my mother got her way and we headed out for the nearby seaside town. We had a relaxed day of paddling and sandcastles, sweets and ice cream were unobtainable, but we managed some fish and chips before heading back to the formidable institute of learning-by-fear. On our return we were informed that in our absence the children had had a rare treat. The housekeeper had somehow been able to acquire enough oranges to give one to each child. Two oranges remained on the mantle-piece in the dinning room, the oranges that would have been given to the two Vaughan children. My mother asked the headmistress if we could have our oranges; however she refused on the grounds that as we were not present when the oranges were distributed we had forfeited our right to have them. In spite of all the pleading and arguing that my mother tried, backed up by our tears and sad faces, our two oranges sat prominently on the mantle-piece for several days. We looked at those oranges with longing, imagining what they must taste like, as we had never tasted one before. Here in another time and another place I could reach out my hand and pluck the juiciest orange directly from the tree.

Every year in Brazil there is the Carnival. Carnival in Rio is of course the most famous, although it is just as much an event for the people in the interior towns and villages and equally exciting. For four days no work gets done, except for the barest and most urgent essentials. The cows were usually milked and the animals fed—well not always. Nothing that could possibly wait for four days was even considered. Every night during the carnival we would go into Pitangueiras and join the festivities. Up country we did not have the elaborate costumes and decorations that are so well known when Rio de Janeiro celebrates Carnival, yet we still had the night-long hypnotic, rhythmic dancing without the necessity of partners, similar to the jumping-up in Trinidad. It was this sort of dancing that changed the style of dancing for youngsters everywhere, the forerunner of the disco dancing.

Young people used a coolant spray; initially they used it to spray other people for fun, which was quite harmless, but the trouble started when they started to spray their handkerchiefs and then sniff the fumes. After a while many of the youngsters went into a drunken stupor, often passing out after a brief spell of erratic and often quite violent behaviour. It was a very cheap way of getting drunk and many of the youngsters were quite sick afterwards. For those who used the spray sparingly, it had the effect of keeping them going all night in a semi stupor, a cheap high. Although I did not use the spray there was enough in the air to increase the hypnotic effect of the constant, basic rhythm of the carnival music. I found that the night had turned to day and I was still full of energy, at least until I got home and fell onto my bed and passed out.

Of course all good things come to an end and Carnival is no exception. The last day of Carnival is followed by the first day of Lent. The Catholic Church has a very strong influence on the lives of the inhabitants of the small interior towns. At the stroke of midnight the bell from the Catholic Church that stood in the main square, boomed out, followed by the amplified voice of the priest.

"It is now Lent you are committing a sin by dancing and drinking." The voice reminded us. "Go back to your homes or you will by damned to eternal hell."

The band stopped in mid note and the revellers rushed for the door. Within minutes the social club, where we were, was an empty shell. Carnival was a great release for the people whose lives were influenced by near poverty and an overbearing church. Lent came as such a stark contrast after those few precious days of joy and freedom.

Pitangueiras, like every other small town in the interior of Brazil, became a virtual ghost town during Lent. Even the Saturday evening ritualistic courting parade round the town square was cancelled for Lent. This parade was the time-honoured way that the young Brazilian singles were able to size each other up as well as show themselves off. The boys walked one way round the square while the girls walked the opposite way, usually in twos or threes, giggling with feigned embarrassment. The boys put on the airs and strutted, pretending—everyone was pretending—not to be interested in the girls' furtive glances. The girls seemed to be in deep conversation, although their eyes were always discretely on the alert.

When a boy and a girl had singled each other out, after several rounds of the square, the girl would usually say to her companion that she was tired and they would sit down on one of the benches. The boy and his companions would decide that they too were tired the next turn round and just happen to find room on the same bench. The other girls and boys in the groups would resume their walk leaving the two would be suitors alone on the bench. If it seems logical that the next move was a roll in the hay, forget it, perhaps a touching of fingers may be possible but no more. Should the friendship continue to the stage where a date was arranged, the evening would be for three. The third person was the girl's mother or perhaps an aunt or grandmother, although usually the mother. The hapless couple was not able to even steal a kiss or hold hands, as the hawkeyed mother was never more than a few feet away.

I used to watch these trios sitting awkwardly in the local cinema or restaurant, nobody knowing what to say or where to look. I first came to experience this awesome phenomenon when I innocently asked a girl out for the evening. I had very little money to spend at the best of times so I brought what I thought and hoped would be more than adequate for the two of us to see a film and have a little something to eat afterwards. To my horror her dragon of a mother came along for the evening. Mother was sitting right behind us in the cinema and then later sat drinking whisky by the glassful while I fumbled through a somewhat awkward conversation in bad Portuguese about the weather or the price of goats in Afghanistan.

The evening came to an abrupt end when my money ran out and I was no longer able to maintain mother's lust for whisky. No man was good enough for her daughter if he could not keep mother in whisky.

After the carnival was over life on Tres Barros came back once more to the normal routine of farm life and I returned to my sick calves plus the other areas of responsibility that were gradually coming my way.

One night Frank woke me with the news that there was a fire in the barn across the field from the house. He was not too concerned but felt we should do something. The barn had been only used for storing fence posts and wire, and was usually only half occupied. Frank's lack of emergency was understandable, though what he did not know was that we had recently decided to use it as a temporary retiro, while one was being repaired. The barn now housed a dozen or so young calves. In seconds DP had been roused and we were all running across the field as fast as we could go. Beyond the barn was a row of workers' houses, so Frank ran over to call for help. All the houses had their shutters closed and doors bolted and it took a lot of banging and explaining before any help came. DP and I opened the barn door and got the poor scared calves out as quickly as we could. We found that the fire was still confined to one part of the barn where there had been some hay stored, and the calves had been able to run to the other end. When we arrived they were gathered in one corner, very frightened but safe. With the help of the workers from the houses we were able to get the fire under control and, by cutting the roof beams and separating the remainder of the barn; we were able to save at least a part of the barn.

Just as the fire was coming under control I remembered that there had been a very sick calf here the last time I had visited and I had not seen him amongst the ones we had saved. He had obviously been too weak to escape the fire and had perished in the blaze. We were able to confirm this the following day when we came across the remains of the poor little fellow in the rubble.

Sometimes I had to go to Pitangueiras for business and when I did I often stopped at a little bar on the outskirts of town, where I was sure to meet my favourite local character. Alfonso was an old man with a weather beaten face that was invariably lit up with a smile that lacked most of its teeth and accompanied by laughter. He seemed to be a very carefree and happy man, although his eyes never lost their habitual alertness. On the few times I saw him walking I noticed that he did so with a distinct limp; one leg had obviously been badly damaged. For a glass of beer or a shot of cachaça he was always good for a story. At first I took his stories with a large pinch of salt, but later when I had heard from other people about this man, I listened with renewed fascination. Alfonso had been one of the early pioneers in this part of Brazil, at a time when it was wild lawless country. He had quite a reputation with a gun and later in his career became a much feared and respected hired killer. As law and order started to infiltrate the interior towns Alfonso's job had become more difficult. He had been forced to flee further in to the interior. After a span of years, some of which he spent in Paraguay, Alfonso returned to Pitangueiras to buy some land with his hard earned money and retire. The people he killed were mainly farmers who were competing for land or water rights. Sometimes his job was to avenge another killing or satisfy a family's honour when a daughter's virginity had been violated. As things got more difficult Alfonso had to restrict his business to high stake killings when he knew that he would have to kill and run. I asked him once if he felt badly about the people he had killed.

"No Senhor", said Alfonso, for just a moment his face was serious. "It was just a job. I never knew the people, they were just contracts."

In the interior of Brazil, killing a man did not seem to be a very serious crime. Stealing a horse or violating a girl's virginity were the most heinous of crimes. I met a professional fisherman on the river who had killed his wife when he had found her with another man. He had been sent to prison for one year.

From time to time we would have cows to sell because we were trying to create a new breed of Red Poll crossed with the local Zebu cattle, to replace the failed Friesian cross. The breed was eventually successful and was known as the Pitangueiras. In order to keep the standards high we had to cull off any cows that did not meet our strict requirements. This meant that there were cows at the various stages of the cross that were of far better quality than the local cattle but were, nevertheless, rejects for the programme.

When we were ready to sell we would let it be known in Pitangueiras. Very quickly the word would spread and many of the local farmers would be interested in buying. If there were no 'take-all' offers prior to the day, we would sell them individually by auction. There was one regular buyer who was always welcome, who had previously worked on Tres Barros. Jun had been working on one of the retiros and had been thrown badly by his horse. He had been sufficiently injured for the company to pay him off. It was often the case that a man who was paid off squandered the money and then became virtually unhireable. Jun had used the money to buy a small piece of land on the outskirts of Pitangueiras. Jun had recovered from his injuries and had started to buy one or two cows from us. He sometimes bought two and resold one for a profit. Gradually he built up his own herd as well as a reputation for being a good and honest dealer. By the time I met Jun he was buying up to a dozen head at a time.

The boiada, crossing a stream.

10

TRAIL BOSS

"You said you wanted to go to Barretos with the boiada." DP suddenly broke his normal silence. "Fernandez has gone sick. You will replace him. We are sending six hundred, leaving tomorrow."

"Replace Fernandez?" I gasped. Fernandez was the Capitaz (foreman). I had mentioned, to DP on a few occasions, my desire to join the boiada for the experience but in his usual manner he had merely grunted. Once he had said, "there is enough for you to do and learn here, without going off to play cowboys for four days." I had let the matter drop.

About once or twice a year, we used to send our steers to the meat factory at Barretos. This particular herd was made up of our own steers, born and raised in Tres Barros. They had matured and fattened in the pasture for four years since being weaned. They were now ready for the ultimate sacrifice. Barretos was about four days away in terms of trailing cattle. A party of four cowboys and a capitaz-in-charge was the usual requirement. This is crazy, I thought. My first real boiada and I was the Boiadeiro (trail boss).

I had been working cattle with Zeze and the boys for over six months by this time, and of course we were always moving cattle from place to place but I was now going to be responsible for six hundred head of cattle for four days.

The following day started early. I drove up with DP to the boundary of the farm, where the cattle had been assembled.

"We'll count them out together and then they are all yours." DP said, as we saddled up. I had had two of my horses brought up the evening before, including Pitangueiras, my favourite.

"Six hundred even," said DP, as we finished counting. I rather nervously concurred. "Make sure there are six hundred when you get there. Count whenever you stop or start, and whenever you feel there could have been any missed," he lectured me. "It is better to count more often than less, and don't be afraid to recount if you are in doubt. He turned his horse and headed back to the retiro.

My eyes lingered on DP for a moment, as he rode away with military bearing, sitting tall in the saddle, like Napoleon reviewing the troops before battle. I turned to realize that the next move was mine. The men and the cattle were, like the cast of a vast film set, waiting for the director to call 'action.' I raised my hand and gave the forward signal. The lead rider sounded his long bullhorn, breaking the early morning quiet with a long, low, plaintive note, and set off down the trail. It only required a few shouts from the rear for the entire boiada to be on the move.

"We must keep them close together, Senhor," suggested Joaquim, the oldest hand. We were several hours down the trail, approaching a small town. The only way past it was right through the main street. "They are less likely to spook if they are close."

All went well as we entered the town. There was very little movement in the almost deserted streets. We only had to pass through the fairly short main street and then turn off at the end, to join up once more with the cattle corridor. As we were coming to the end of the town, suddenly a bell rang out, heralding a crisis. School was let out and all hell broke loose. Our well-behaved steers were suddenly confronted with a mob of excited children, celebrating their moment of liberation. The chase was on, up side streets into people's yards, to the accompaniment of the children's delighted cheers. It was a cattleman's nightmare, as the herd fragmented.

I spurred my horse and joined the melee, hot in pursuit of a group of steers that were heading for the church. Beyond the charging steers I saw the church door open, and the village priest appeared, with an inquisitive but benevolent smile on his face, perhaps wondering what the noise was all about.

"Get back Father!" I yelled. The smile froze as he confronted, eyeball to eyeball, several tons of frightened beef seeking refuge. The huge door slammed just in time to separate priest from beast.

It took an hour to glue the herd back together again. Once we were well into the corridor and clear of the town, I decided that we must make a count.

"Joaquim!" I called, "would you help me count?" His weather-beaten face seemed to pale just a tinge. The eyes, usually inscrutably hard, showed a hint of hurt, just before he lowered them.

"I cannot count cattle, Senhor," was the surprise answer.

"Pedro. How about you?" Pedro grinned sheepishly as he shook his head.

"Eucledes? Joao?" I got the same response from both of them.

That may seem strange but counting cattle is considered to be quite an art, and it also brings with it the odour of responsibility. Cattle go past very quickly once the herd starts to move. It is difficult to keep count with large numbers, so we used hand counters to click off each fifty. The trick is to count only one part of a steer, usually the head, to avoid counting the same steer twice. There is no time for the second look. Steers tend to bunch up and rush through together. There is only time for an impression of a steer passing, as you keep your eyes fixed in one direction.

So I, the least experienced member of the group, and probably for hundreds of miles around, had the sole responsibility of counting the cattle each time, and arriving in Barretos with the right number. I counted the herd twice, just to be sure, and felt confident that all six hundred had in fact traversed the town together.

"Let the cattle walk at a grazing speed'. Zeze had taught me well.

"On a long walk the cattle can lose a lot of weight if you push them. They should be able to walk as if they were wandering around the pasture looking for a good tuft of grass," he would explain. Where the grass was sparse, as it often was along a well-used cattle corridor, it was possible to keep them moving a little faster but still calmly and quietly.

We were going through fairly well used corridors, and in many areas the grass was almost non-existent, so we were able to keep a reasonable pace. We were on the first day of a trail and the cattle were fresh off a fattening pasture, comfortably far from starving. Although they were in no immediate danger of losing weight, just the same it was still essential to find pasture along the way. Each night we rented a paddock, or small pasture, from a farmer. As this was a heavily used trail, what pastures were available were pitifully short on grass.

Four star hotels were also in short supply along the way, and usually the best we could do, if we were lucky, was to sling our hammocks in a cow shed. For a price, the farmer's wife would produce rice and beans with perhaps a little dried beef, and the inevitable thick, black, very sweet coffee, with more of the same for breakfast.

After dinner on the first night, we went down to the corral where we were to sleep. There was a small calf pen at one end of the corral that was the only shelter. We hung our hammocks from the rafters and after a little light hearted banter prepared to sleep. Well all except Joaquim who realized, as he unsaddled his horse that he had left his hammock behind. The truth might have been that he did not have one and was ashamed to admit it. He ended up sleeping draped across a wheelbarrow. I slept well that night and hardly gained consciousness even when a rat ran down my hammock rope, across my face, jumped off my chest and landed squarely on Joaquim. He tried to hit it but only managed to tip over his wheelbarrow.

I woke early the next morning to find that a hungry calf was eagerly suckling my fingers. I was drifting awake to the rather erotic sensation when the calf became frustrated by the lack of milk and butted me hard to get it flowing. After a breakfast that seemed to be the left over from the night before, we prepared to get moving again. The horses were lined up for saddling: this was done by stringing a lasso across the corral. With a little urging the horses took their places, lined up abreast, with their chests just touching the lasso. This was a standard training, which, out in the open field, was a great saving. The horses would stand quietly with their heads over the lasso while we checked them for any cuts, swelling or ticks and then chose the horses we needed for the day. We always took spare horses on a long trail.

Day succeeded day, as the sun baked Brazilian landscape drifted slowly by. Cattle trails, quite logically, take a route that stays, wherever possible, well away from the mainstream. With the exception of that one town we only passed the occasional little farmhouse, or worker's cottage—where the wife and perhaps the half-naked children, would stop what they were doing and come to the edge of the garden and greet us.

Sometimes fresh water was offered, or a cup of coffee, whilst the local gossip was exchanged. We were their link with the outside world, and the cowboys relished their role as storytellers, adding further embellishments for each captive audience.

The news was usually local, though the 'Ingles' would nearly always become the object of their curiosity and the same men who had so recently laughed at my attempts at becoming a cowboy, were now telling stories that made me out to be a legendary hero of the Brazilian west. Who was I to deny the legend as it unfolded and developed?

The dry, searing heat was not made any more pleasant by two thousand four hundred hooves stirring the dust. The cowboy's kerchief tied to protect the nose and mouth came into its own, especially when you were bringing up the rear of the herd. The slow rhythm of a walking horse, coupled with the glaring heat, can be most soporific. Eucledes was obviously well away, head resting on his chest and the handle of his whip draped across his shoulder, with the long leather end wriggling its way through the dust twenty feet behind his horse.

With a theatrical, conspiratorial wink, Pedro, the youngest member, always ready for a joke, edged his horse directly behind the sleeping man. The whip's end had a will of its own, and jumped sideways each time Pedro's horse's hoof was about to catch it. We watched in silent anticipation. Eucledes was blissfully unaware of the drama that was occurring behind him. The hoof finally caught its prey, the whip sprung taut, the handle leaped into life, knocking Eucledes' hat high into the air. Eucledes almost leapt off his horse with shock, whilst Pedro nearly fell off his laughing.

As we neared the factory holding farm, on our final day, we had to pass near the railway line for a few hundred yards.

"If we can get past this section without a train coming, we are safe," murmured Joaquim, scanning the tracks in either direction. All was peaceful, the air was still, and the cattle, well accustomed to the routine by now, were closing the gap to their final resting-place. I was nervously holding my breath. The railway flanked the trail on one side at this point, and some rather scrubby, unfenced undergrowth flanked the other side.

The quiet was suddenly broken by the piercing screech of a train's whistle, followed by the rhythmic pounding of metal wheels crossing the track joints. A flock of birds, startled by the sudden noise, rose screeching from the bushes and the cattle, like a shoal of fish, turned as one, and ran.

"Don't let them reach the bushes." I yelled rather pointlessly, as the herd was already heading for cover at full gallop.

By the time the train had thundered its way past, there was not a single head of steer in the open. Finding six hundred frightened steers, playing hide and seek in dense bushes, is not a game for the faint hearted.

Gradually we persuaded the clusters of steers we found, back onto the path but a few individuals had become separated. Frightened animals snorted and cried out as they struggled to free themselves from the bushes and return to the herd. They were alone and scared and could not see the other cattle.

Eucledes and Joao remained with the herd on the path, whilst Joaquim, Pedro and I went in search of our runaways. After following one of the steers into dense bush, I found myself separated from the others and surrounded by thick, impenetrable brush. I found my quarry caught in the undergrowth. There was no way for him to go on, and I stood in the way of his retreat. I was unable to get behind him to urge him out. I reversed my horse in towards him shouting and cracking the whip near his face. He began to snort, eyes staring, head twitching. He lowered his head and charged. I spurred my horse, keeping clear of those horns. He managed a twenty yard-burst before stopping, apparently quite overcome by his own show of bravado. The fear and bewilderment soon returned, so I quickly backed up and provoked him again. He responded quicker than I expected, and I felt the impact as his head ploughed into the fleshy buttocks of my horse, who responded with a swift kick, that left the poor steer dazed. Luckily he did not have the long horns of the Zebu. While the steer was still blinking, I got between him and the bushes, just as Pedro joined me with a small group of runaways. My escapee was soon back amongst friends.

Once we had collected the herd and returned to the trail, we were close to the receiving corral, so I did the final count there with the receiving capitaz.

"Six-hundred even," announced the receiver without emotion, yet my heart was still pounding, for fear that we had left some in the bushes. I turned my horse and rode over to the team and announced in as steady a voice as I could muster. "All correct, we can go home now". I rode tall in the saddle as we left the corral. I had become a man, a leader looked up to by the very men who had taught me, and the feeling was good.

11

FRED

After the thirty-minute drive from Campo Grande on my recent trip to Brazil, Rod Paxton announced that we were now entering Fazenda Estrela and I knew without a doubt that this was indeed what I had known as Ligacao. The road, once we had left the main highway, was the same dirt road that I had known forty years before although the landscape was certainly more lush and green, with clear, open pastures stretching in every direction. As we swung into the sede, it was as if time had stood still. My house, or what had been my house, awaited me at the top of the rise. It stood alone as bleak as I had first known it, with no sign of the garden that I had tried to form. As we swept past, a flood of memories flashed through my mind. The most vivid of these was a bittersweet memory of my beloved dog Fred. It was here that his short life tragically ended. I could feel once more the awful moment when, after a nightlong vigil, I knew that my constant and loyal companion was gone. As I looked around the sede happier moments pierced the momentary gloom. There was where he often sat waiting for me to come home. There was the tree under which he would lie when I was working in the office. I then remembered the moment when Fred and I first met all those years ago in Tres Barros.

Loneliness was by far the greatest enemy of the single assistant manager: The creature comforts were not entirely lacking. The assistant's bungalow on Tres Barros was typical of most; they were far from luxurious, usually simply furnished, with the barest essentials. Because land was not in short supply on the farms our houses were usually set in a garden easily the size of a football field. Even in the most sumptuous setting though, living alone can be hard to take. The work on the farm was demanding, and sometimes it kept me away from the house from sunrise until sunset or even later it was invariably the dread of a lonely house that made me find extra things to do. In the isolated parts of Brazil, like Mato Grosso, there was of course very little in the way of entertainment. Television and radio were only found in the main cities, and I had no hi-fi or records. English books were impossible to buy, and there were no newspapers or magazines. Sundays or rainy days were black days on my calendar.

It was in Tres Barros that Fred entered my life. Tres Barros did have a reasonable social life and I shared the bachelors' house with DP and Frank, so it was not through loneliness that I agreed to adopt a puppy. I remembered having an Alsatian when we had stayed on a farm as a child, during the war years. After my father had been called up for active service, my mother tried various jobs to keep things going. After the unpleasantness of the school she took a job as secretary to the owner of a large farm. The owner's Alsatian had puppies and she gave us one. The puppy adored my brother and I and we him. That puppy was one of the few happy memories that survived the dreary war years. I had often, over the years, dreamed of having an Alsatian of my own.

A dog has often been described as man's best friend. Fred certainly lived up to that description during those early years in Brazil. He was just a little black and tan ball of fluff when we first met, fitting nicely into my two cupped hands: a pitiful little thing crying for his mother's milk. At the ripe old age of about one and a half months, totally against his will, Fred experienced one of life's great traumas—expulsion from mother's nest and separation from the litter. It is a cruel blow for any being and all the coochi-cooing in the world won't lessen the pain. It was hard to imagine that this scared little puppy, was a much feared and respected Alsatian and yet he was. Even Attila the Hun must have wet his diapers at some stage.

The first few weeks were interspersed with cuddling, licking, lots of biting with those oh-so-sharp little teeth, and of course, clearing up messes; often just before DP discovered them—sometimes very shortly after. The name Fred did not come from the Bassett Hound of the same name but through total lack of imagination on my part. Perhaps the fact that my uncle used to call the family cat Fred had some an influence.

Fred started to grow feet first, followed by the tail, and then the ears. Alsatian puppies are about the most cowardly of animals, and Fred was no exception. I took Fred in the camionette to one of the retiros, when he was almost fully-grown. On our arrival a skinny little mutt came out of the corral, barking like a banshee. I turned round expecting to see my fearsome German Shepherd putting a stop to the nonsense but he was nowhere to be found. It took half an hour of patient coaxing, to get him out from under some timbers. Somehow the timid little puppy turned into a dog, although much more than just a four-legged tail-wagger. Fred and I became an inseparable team.

Life started early on the farm, though never early enough for Fred. The morning started for me at 5.30 am, with an impatient bark from the door, usually enough to render further sleep out of the question. After five minutes, if I had managed to fall back to sleep, peace was further shattered by another bark, this time close to my ear. Sundays were no exception but after a few clashes of wills, we would come to a compromise and I would get up for a while, then sneak back to bed. One morning I woke to find that I was feeling quite ill, just the flu, it turned out, although bad enough to put me out of action for the day. Fred returned for the follow up bark; instead of shattering my eardrums, he came over and touched my nose with his. Arriving at a diagnosis and convinced that I was not malingering, Fred sat down next to the bed and kept a vigil for the whole day. The following morning he approached the bed first, decided that I was fit to work, and let me have the full wake-up treatment.

Fred soon proved his worth with cattle; he had an instinctive knowledge of herding. The name German Shepherd was not given lightly and he was able to make a worthwhile contribution whenever I was involved in moving or sorting cattle. Often, when I was sorting in the corral, with too few men for the job, Fred would take the gate. He would sit by the open gate, only allowing the sorted cattle to pass. Fred would rarely let the wrong one past. His record would match the best horseman on the farm.

When trailing cattle Fred would always patrol the flank, often alone, keeping an eye on the column, ready to herd a straggler back into line. A steer broke loose one day, when we were returning a herd to an out-lying pasture, after being vaccinated against foot and mouth disease. Fred was a little distance behind him when the runaway, finding himself alone, panicked and ran. Fred raced through the shoulder high grass, angling to cut him off before he got too far out into the open ground. The steer was in full flight, eyes wide with fear, tail pointing to the sky. Fred closed in on his prey and lunged, grabbing the steer by the nose. A cloud of dust, punctuated by legs, tail and horns, cleared to reveal both animals lying motionless, still joined by the nose and teeth. I brought my horse round, placing the steer between the herd and myself. Nervously, I looked to see how much damage my dog had done; rehearsing in my mind, how I was going to explain to DP, how my dog had bitten off a steer's nose. There were no obvious signs of blood, but the steer was lying very still and attentive; so was my dog, who had the steer's full and undivided attention. With my whip ready to crack, I called Fred. He let go and jumped back. The steer, none the worse from the encounter, stood up, looking bewildered and far from amused. There was not a scratch mark to be seen. I have no idea how Fred learnt that manoeuvre. He certainly did not get it from me.

The fact that I spent a lot of time on horseback, with Fred running alongside, meant that he had to follow my commands. I had always talked to Fred, dramatising my emotions and he seemed to be able to tune in to my thoughts.

Dogs want to please their masters though all too often they do not know what pleases and what does not. The sound of my angry voice was a far greater and more effective deterrent than pain. Fred never knew the feel of a stick, nor was he ever chained. Once the basic words of command had been learned, Fred could be relied on to obey without question.

Fred's graduation came one day when I was inspecting fences and watering holes, alone. I found that a section of the fence had been broken, and the herd was milling around the opening. I got the cattle back on the side where they belonged but as they had been fairly scattered, I wanted to make sure that none had made it to the river. The fence was where it was, because of a rather dangerous part of the river where we had lost cattle before. I told Fred to sit and stay at the gap in the fence, while I explored the riverbank. I rode off, and sure enough, found one steer in trouble trying to swim against the current. It took quite a long time to get my lasso onto the steer, pull him to the bank, and then guide him back to the fence. I had been completely out of Fred's sight for most of the time, yet, when I returned he was still sitting exactly where I had left him. The cattle were gathered closely round him, inspecting this strange little animal although they were still on their side of the fence. I called Fred, telling him by my tone, how very pleased I was. Together we eased the stray through the fence, and I set to, to make a temporary repair of the hole; making a note to send someone out the following day to do a better job.

Fred soon became my constant assistant and companion. He was never more than a few feet away from me, day and night. It became a great joy to work cattle with a horse that knew the business, and a dog that had a natural instinct, and did what he was told. Although Fred became a rugged cattle dog, he was very gentle, and was a great favourite with the children, who loved playing with him.

The farms manager, Roddy Taylor was visiting one day from head office. We were engrossed in an inspection of some of the better Red Poll cross cows and their calves. Roddy turned round to find my Alsatian devouring one the cowboy's children. Roddy ran to save the little boy from an untimely end. I called Fred to release the child, who sat up smiling from ear to ear and pulled Fred down into another wrestle hold.

On that same trip I was showing Roddy Taylor some of the selected cross-breed heifers. We had walked a fair way from the camionette, to get a close look. Cattle tend to be very curious of small animals, and they were crowding round Fred, who was feeling a little threatened. When the cattle got too close for comfort, Fred barked, which sent them running back a few feet.

The disturbance obviously annoyed my VIP, so I pointed to the camionette and told Fred to go back. He trotted off, probably quite glad to be out of there, and on reaching the truck looked round at me. I shouted, "get up," and he jumped into the back and then, "stay," and he waited there until we had finished our examination. Roddy was highly impressed, and I was humbly proud.

One night a capitaz, foreman, from a transiting boiada, came to the house in the evening to ask me if he could use one of the small paddocks, to secure his cattle over night. This was quite a common request and there was no problem. It was late evening and the man stood in the drive outside my house, and clapped his hands, as was the custom. Fred barked at the intruder but fell silent when I came out to talk to the capitaz. We spoke for a few moments, just pleasantries mainly, and the boiadeiro was about to leave, when I noticed that Fred had quietly crept out into the garden, made a wide circuit, and placed himself in a crouch position, a few feet behind the unsuspecting visitor. I am sure that if that man had made a wrong move, he would have been sorry. When the boiadeiro became aware of his predicament, his hand went automatically towards his gun. I reassured him that he was in no danger, as long as he made no sudden moves. That man walked back to his horse so softly, that even his spurs were silent.

Tragedy nearly struck one day when we were spraying the cattle against the ticks and Warble fly that were a constant problem. Fred had been collecting some ticks, and I had spent a good deal of time in the evenings ridding him of them. It was a losing battle, as they were ever present in the grass.

"Give him a spray." Zeze suggested. "There won't be any harm." So saying, he turned the hose onto Fred. We finished spraying the herd and sent the cattle back to the pasture. I finished up in the office and prepared to drive home. Fred looked a little off colour, so I drove past one of the small lakes that were used for irrigation and coaxed Fred into the water, hoping to wash off the spray. When we arrived home, I fed him with milk, to detoxify him and then kept him in the house as cool as possible.

Fred started to go down hill rapidly. His breathing became laboured, and his eyes took on the panicked look of a seriously ill dog. I lay on the floor beside him trying to comfort him. Suddenly his breathing became desperate. He was fighting for each breath—then to my horror it stopped, his eyes became fixed, and all four legs were rigid in front of him. The heart had stopped. I rammed my fist into the Solar Plexus and pumped. After a few pumps there was some reaction, and the lungs, which were fully inflated, deflated. The breathing was not returning, so I breathed for him for perhaps half an hour, not mouth to mouth but by pressure on the chest. Sometimes he took over, and then stopped. At times he breathed weakly and I lent a little assistance. I lay most of that night, with my arm lightly across Fred's chest, monitoring each intake of air. The crisis was over although Fred was a very sick dog for several days. I am convinced that it was this episode that brought about his early death a year later.

12

TRANSFER TO MATO GROSSO

When I got my transfer orders to go to Mato Grosso, Fred suddenly became a bit of a problem. I was to fly to Campo Grande, the Capital of the State of Mato Grosso do Sul, which was a few hours drive from Fazenda Ligacao, where I was to be stationed. On the Monday there was a flight from Barretos, and on Wednesday from Ribeirao Preto, both towns being about three hours drive from Tres Barros although in opposite directions. I set off for Barretos in good time, bags in the back of the camionette. Fred and I sat up front next to Nogeiro, the chief clerk and sometimes driver for the Browns. I cringed in agony as I watched Nogeiro jamming the gears into place, with an accompaniment of Portuguese profanity and the ominous noise of grinding cogs. I had nursed that camionette and eased the gears, with a tender loving touch. It just took a light pressure at the right time to ease the gear into place. I winced each time we changed gear, and there was a lot of gear changing during the three-hour drive. Nogeiro dumped me at the airport, and with a farewell crash of gears, sped off on the return trip.

"Dogs need to be crated." I was informed, as I tried to arrange passage for the two of us. I argued with the official, who merely shrugged his shoulders. I asked for the manager who also shrugged his shoulders, and then when the plane was at the gate, I demanded to see the pilot. I was led out onto the tarmac and introduced to a face peering from the cockpit of the DC 4 aircraft. I made my plea, pointing out the urgency of my journey, the distance I would have to travel to return to the farm, and the fact that there was no means of transport. "He is a very gentle dog." I assured him. He looked down at my pony-sized Alsatian, who chose that moment to start barking. My shushing was too late. The pilot turned a shade paler, and shook his head before withdrawing it back into the cockpit.

With no transport, no telephone, and a lot of open country between the farm and Barretos airport, I was at a loss as to what to do. As I was walking back to the airport building, I noticed one of the 'teko tekos,' taxi planes, and so walked over to see if it was for hire. A tall youthful character dressed in jeans and a tee shirt was tinkering with something under the Cessna's instrument panel; he straightened out as I approached.

"Is this plane for hire?" I asked.

"Where do you want to go?" asked the young man, who looked as if he had just come away from a college basketball match. I told him where I was going and assured him that there was an airport, neglecting to tell him that there hadn't been a plane land on it since I had been on the farm. The grass had been several feet high when I last looked. We walked into the airport building to consult a map, and then file a flight plan. A few minutes later Fred and I were racing down the runway in our own private plane.

It was a fascinating flight, over the country that I had crossed, both by horseback with the boiada and vehicle for the occasional weekends. The countryside slipped below us like a huge quilted carpet, done in shades of green and brown. After a delightful twenty-minute flight, we located the neighbouring town of Pitangueiras, and then followed the road to the centre of Fazenda Tres Barros. The pilot gave me a strange look, as we made a pass over the airstrip. The grass was even higher than I had remembered it. After a couple of passes the pilot crossed himself, and started to mutter something, then turned in for the approach. There could have been a dozen giant anthills hidden in that grass, happily luck was with us and we made a bumpy yet safe landing.

Both DP and Mr. Brown, looking a little concerned, arrived in separate vehicles, expecting to see the General Manager at least, and possibly even 'heaven forbid,' Mr. Vestey himself.

"What the hell are you doing here?" DP had a way with words. I explained my dilemma, and suggested that the pilot be paid, as I had no money. Mr. Brown sent Nogeira, who had just returned from Barretos, back to the sede to fetch the money. As soon as the pilot had counted it and found it all there, he climbed back aboard and started his engines. The three of us stood and watched, as the plane roared back into the sky, once more missing the many bumps and anthills that must have been on the strip.

The carpenter was put to work to make a crate in time to get me onto the Wednesday's plane from Ribeirao Preto. It was quite obvious from the outset that Fred did not approve of his latest method of travel. There were disapproving looks when I put him into the crate just prior to the flight. He obeyed though he obviously had no intention of staying there for long. When I arrived at Campo Grande Airport, in Mato Grosso do Sul, after a three-hour flight, I became aware of a rather tense scene at the tail end of the aeroplane. Baggage handlers and ground staff were clustered at the bottom of the steps leading to the baggage compartment, staring up with obvious concern. As I reached the steps I saw the object of their consternation. There stood Fred, framed by the freight hatch, with his ears cocked, eyes glaring at the airport staff, with a slight upward curl of his lips, daring anyone to approach; a picture of raw, animal confrontation. To the obvious consternation of all the onlookers, I ran up the steps, to be greeted by an enthusiastic lick and a lot of tail wagging; peace had returned to the world. One glance inside the aircraft was enough to see what had happened to the crate. It was shattered and had been distributed evenly around the hold. I decided to donate the remains to whoever wanted it, and led my faithful and much relieved dog across the tarmac to meet my new manager.

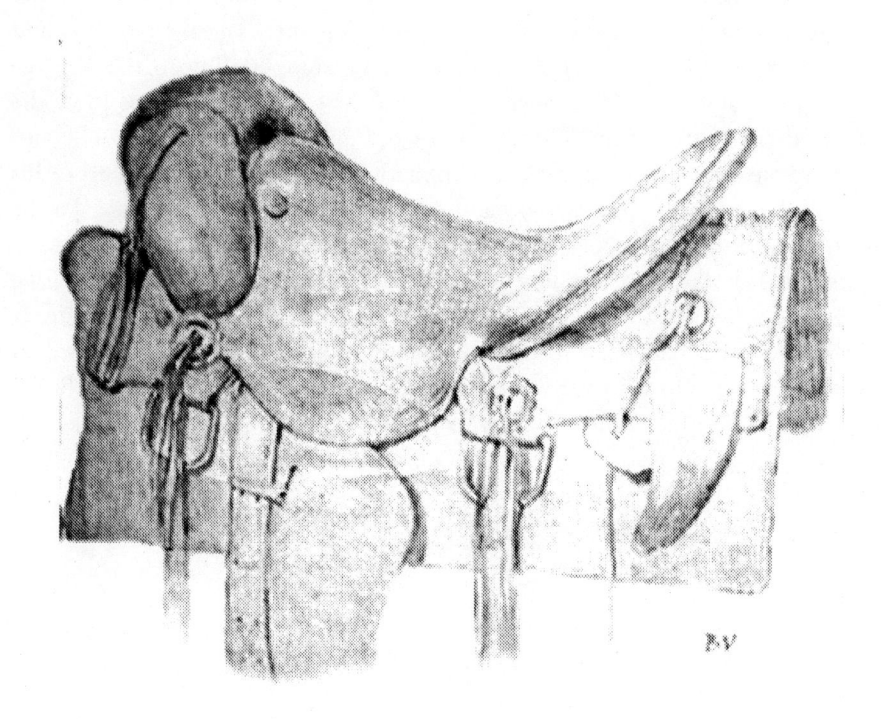

My saddle.

13

LIFE ON THE OPEN RANGE

Peter Richardson, my new manager and his wife Shirley, met me at the airport and drove me, after a brief stop in Campo Grande, to the fazenda. I took a liking to the couple right from the start. He was of a slim build, with a stooped posture, head always pushed forwards as if it felt that the body was not moving fast enough. Peter was obviously a well-educated man who could have passed for a university lecturer, yet he possessed an enthusiastic energy that was infectious. Shirley was an uncomplicated girl-next-door who had met Peter when they were both very young and wanted nothing more than to be where he was. She was always very kind to me, as they both were and I felt at ease in their presence.

My most vivid memory of that fascinating drive, so different from the one from Pitangueiras to Tres Barros, was when we were within sight of the sede. As we crossed the river a welcoming party of six or seven Rheas met us. They escorted us for a quarter of a mile, running alongside us a little to the right, until we approached the milking corral. Rheas are similar to the Australian Emus. They could easily keep ahead of the jeep even when it was going up to about forty miles per hour. This particular flock could always be seen somewhere fairly close to the sede, so I got to know them well.

Fazenda Ligacao, unlike Tres Barros where there were many small clusters of houses and retiros dotted around the farm, was very centralized. The sede, homestead, was the centre and focal point of the farm. A large rectangle formed by the corral, office, work sheds and a pleasant little house where the bookkeeper lived made up the central part of the sede. The manager's house set in a very beautiful garden and the far more basic assistant's house; mine, made up the northern border. Other stables and sheds, as well as the scattered workers' houses, divided by a small stream, were on the western end. That same stream curled round and made up the southern boundary of the sede. The milking retiro, corral and paddocks were to the east. Beyond this little ecosystem there was nothing for miles. There was one other division, called Cervo at the far end of the farm, which was run by a rather secretive, locally employed German manager. It was a large area and so treated as a separate division. I'll say more about the manager later.

Space had been no problem in planning the layout of the sede, so there was plenty of open ground between the various buildings. The main corral and the milking corral were separate from each other and built well away from the houses. Cattle milling around in the corral stirred up a lot of dust, especially in the dry season. When we were working the cattle there, a dust cloud would hang over the corral. It did not take much of a wind for the dust to spread over the houses, in spite of the distance.

Life on Fazenda Ligacao was totally different to what I had become used to on Tres Barros. The area was vast,—the whole of Tres Barros could have fitted into one of the campos (large pastures)—it was semi-desert, with sparse, coarse grass growing amongst the stunted apologies for trees. Wild life, in many forms, abounded though mostly away from the inhabited area.

The Richardsons had already been based in Mato Grosso for a few years.

They both knew the place and the life well and in spite of the remoteness seemed to enjoy it. Although Peter was to be my manager, he was also one of the company's cattle buyers and spent long periods, when the weather made it possible, up in the Pantanal area, buying herds of cattle from the many, often isolated, small farms there. The wet season in the Pantanal caused such flooding that farms could be cut off for months on end. Once the water receded, Peter would buy and assemble boiadas of young thin steers, thin because pasture was scarce, which would be walked for weeks to reach Ligacao. During the buying season I saw very little of Peter. Shirley used to go down to Sao Paulo during this period, so I would be alone. I did get to know them enough to like them and enjoy their company. Peter Richardson, so easily recognized, even from a distance because of his thin slightly stooped stature, accentuated by a wide rather floppy hat, was a man of boundless energy and gave the appearance of being able to rush-off-in-all-directions at the same time. As he emerged from his house in the morning, usually at a more gentlemanly hour, the rather relaxed atmosphere around the sede suddenly became charged with his energy. Even the cattle seemed to take more notice. Peter looked for perfection and gave no quarter. Shirley, his wife, spent some time each day in the office acting as Peter's secretary and he would order her around as if she were an eighteen-year old from typing pool. Shirley took it all in her stride, knowing that in the house she was the boss.

My new home, the assistant's house, was a small bungalow with a rather bare garden but with a commanding view of the entire sede, the entry road and bridge, and then a vast expanse of land stretching for miles beyond the river. Immediately in front of the bungalow was an open paddock, part of which I later fenced off for my garden. Behind the house there were some mature trees and then, stretching along the brow of the rise beyond, the airstrip—Peter's gateway to the Pantanal.

I felt somewhat daunted by the prospect of settling in to a house alone. I had no link with the outside world, nor radio or telephone. I could not expect any visitors to drop in for tea. I would not even be able to pop out and buy a newspaper. English language books or magazines were virtually impossible to buy in Campo Grande so that my reading was limited to what I could borrow from the Richardsons, which was in itself also limited. The house itself was not small by normal urban standards; it would have been a pleasant little family house in any town. There were two bedrooms, a sitting room and a large kitchen with a storeroom. A wide veranda looked over what I hoped would be my garden.

My fifteen months of breeding experience were somewhat wasted in Ligacao. The only breeding there consisted of either wild herds, left alone to breed out in the campos, or a few dozen cows kept at the sede for our own dairy purposes. My education in the real business of cattle ranching was however now just beginning. Similar to Tres Barros my education was left to the capitaz, this time in the form of Sebastiao. Sebastiao was a hard, lean, proud almost arrogant man in his fifties, who was in charge of all the cattle on the farm, with the exception of the milking herd. Once more I joined the team of cowboys. Here they were a genuine commitiva, the range cowboys; a very superior race of beings, who looked down with contempt on the vaceiros (breeding cowboys) and even more so, the lowly field workers.

Our day started early; as soon as the foremen of the various departments had met at the office each morning to receive orders, things began. As the commitiva was not involve in milking, we would mount up and be on our way by the time the warming rays of the sun were lighting the tops of the trees. In Tres Barros we had only been able to do our work between morning and afternoon milkings: here we were able to work all day. Sometimes it could be several days before we returned, especially when we went out in the areas called Ligacao and Pontal, at the two opposite extremes east and west. Ligacao was a huge area of wild scrubland. A river formed a boundary on two sides as it made a wide bend. A wedge shaped area of thick virgin jungle, made a natural division between two parts of the fazenda, leaving a relatively short boundary of fencing. The whole area was many square miles of uncultivated, rugged campos. The herds of Zebu, mostly Nelore cattle that lived there were rounded up and inspected a few times a year. The cattle were quite wild, having little contact with humans and so were unused to being handled.

Handling Mato Grosso cattle was a very different technique to what I had known in Tres Barros, where most of the steers had been raised from calves and so had been handled consistently from the time they were born. In Mato Grosso the cattle were mostly raised out in the field and many of them lived a long time before even seeing a man. When we went out into the larger campos we tried to round up as many as we could and then do what ever was needed, there and then. We were prepared for branding and castrating as well as first aid, should we find any of the cattle with sores or wounds.

I did not feel like a total green horn on my first day with the commitiva. I rode my horse as they did, sitting relaxed in the saddle with my toes merely resting in the long stirrups. I spoke their language and could handle a lasso as well as the essential long whip. Our first job after a long ride out to Felipe, one of the large campos towards Ligacao, was to locate the herd. After a little searching we found a small herd resting in the shade of some trees.

"Go with Leonardo," Sebastiao ordered in a whisper. "Make a long swing and come up from behind them. We must get them out into the clear." Leonardo and I walked our horses off to the left until we were out of sight, and then swung back in a wide circle to get into position. Sebastiao and the others selected a clearing and with a scissors action we slowly drove them out of the bushes into the open. While two of the men collected some wood and started a fire, Sebastiao, keeping a good distance from the wary animals, quietly inspected the herd. After a while Sebastiao returned.

"There are four unbranded and two to castrate," he announced.

We waited for the fire to get hot enough before putting the branding iron into the embers, at the same time gently keeping the herd in the clearing. The branding iron has to be almost red hot, so that a quick thrust will leave a clean brand. Properly done there is no wounding or bleeding as the blood vessels are nicely cauterized. If the iron is not hot enough it has to be held longer and the skin becomes cooked. This can result in an area of damaged tissue surrounding the brand. Quite often the wound goes bad, causing suffering to the animal and making the brand illegible.

Claudio, the oldest of the commitiva, prepared his lasso and then slowly and quietly rode towards the herd. Sebastiao stayed by the fire, ready to run over with the branding iron. The rest of us fanned out and encircled the small herd. Claudio pointed at one of the older calves to indicate which one he was going for first. Those of us close to where Claudio was, started to gently urge the herd towards him. As they started to move, Claudio began to swing his lasso and with an effortless, practiced swing, neatly placed the noose around the young animal's head. Working as a team, the horse held the tension on the lasso so that the rider was able to run across to throw the calf. There was a swirl of red dust and then the calf lay, protesting loudly, immobilized by a cord that bound his legs together.

"Esta Pronto." Claudio yelled. Two of the men dismounted and helped to hold the calf still, while Sebastiao grabbed the red-hot iron and ran across to put the company's '&' brand on the flat area of the animal's left cheek. Placing the iron aside for a moment, Sebastiao reach behind him and brought out the castrating pinchers. Moments later the young bull calf was a steer.

There were two methods used for castrating each one had its followers. The first was the method we used in Tres Barros on the young calves that could be watched and cared for, should it be required. This was the total castration with a sharp knife. The scrotum is pulled down and the tip cut off, then each testicle is separated from its sheath and held in one hand while the other hand locates the spermatic chord and exposes it sufficiently to make a clean cut. Obviously the blood supply is also severed before the entire testicle is removed. There is some bleeding, though usually not much, as the arteries tend to constrict themselves. As the incision is quite small healing is usually quick. Rarely did we have to treat the calves for infection. I saw only a few with maggots but they usually tended to be the more sickly animals.

The method that we used in the campos of Mato Grosso was not as sure-fire but many of the animals were much older by the time we were able to castrate them and as follow-up treatment was difficult, it was therefore a better method. We used a large pair of pinchers; designed so that they did not actually close completely, however hard you squeezed. In this way the more delicate spermatic chord was severed yet the more resilient skin was not cut. His meant that there was no exposure to the outside and so no infection. There were some cases where the arteries did not constrict and so internal bleeding took place. Some times a steer that had been castrated this way became the proud father of a string of calves.

After we had dealt with the calves Sebastiao had selected, we took another look at the entire herd to check for any signs of injury or infection.

"There's an open abscess on that old cow there," Leonardo called out, pointing at a rather ancient cow whose bones seemed about to burst through the skin.

"Put her down," called Sebastiao. Leonardo, who already had the lasso in his hand, was able to get the old lady by the horns. As there was no need to contain the herd any more, we all dismounted and helped to throw the ageing cow without causing her any further injury.

The first aid out in the field usually consisted of the occasional wound that had gone bad; sometimes they became infested with maggots. We had to throw the animal and hold him down, in order to clean out the wound and kill the maggots with a special black fluid, which had an antiseptic mixed into a tar base. This was to help to heal the wound as well as to keep the wound free from the flies for as long as possible. Abscesses were quite common, often the result of a Warble fly lava that had died under the skin. If they were ripe we could find the thin spot in the skin and lance it, cleaning out all the pus. It would of course happen on it's own although it was better if we could do it. A streak of pus would attract the flies and often caused the wound to ulcerate or become full of maggots from the fly's eggs.

We spent the day rounding up other small herds of cattle and going through the same procedure. It was getting late when we finished however none of us wished to make camp for the night. We would get back to the sede after dark but we could at least sleep in our own beds. As we were leaving Felipe, Sebastiao spotted a lone cow lying half-hidden behind some scrub. More ominously we saw two vultures perched in a tree just beyond her.

"Senhor Bruce, go with Leonardo and check it out," he ordered. "She might have been hurt or just given birth."

We rode over to take a look and found a calf half delivered. I jumped from my horse and edged closer. There seemed to be no movement from the calf that was still within the sac and the cow looked exhausted. "Keep her occupied," I said to Leonardo. I dived forwards and grabbed the sac, breaking it. The calf started to struggle as I pulled. I was an instant mid-wife and delivered a healthy young female calf. The rest of the commitiva joined us just in time for the happy event.

"We had better take them back with us," Sebastiao decided. If we were not too far away from the sede when we came across a newly born calf or a cow that was just about to give birth, we would try to get them back to a pasture close to the sede, so that the calf could be cared for. We lost many calves at birth out in the campos, as the vultures would attack a newly born calf and pick out its eyes even as it was being born. A young calf was of course fair game to any predator and there were some wild cats and jaguars around.

In theory it was quite easy to persuade a cow with a newborn calf to follow you. You just have to catch the calf and put it across your saddle and ride on home. Catching the calf is fairly easy but avoiding the horns of the angry mother is a different matter. It takes a little teamwork and some fast footwork.

In this case we had the edge. The calf was only minutes old and the cow was exhausted. However we allowed both the cow and her calf a little time to get acquainted.

It was the young, ever enthusiastic Joao's turn to be the hero this time and he waited for his opportunity and then scooped up the little calf and ran, just ahead of the now very mobile cow, and handed it to Leonardo, who was in the saddle and waiting nearby. The rest of us had our hands full keeping the cow away from her calf and then man who was holding it. Leonardo, with one wary eye on the now furious cow, laid the calf gently onto the thick sheepskin that covered his saddle. The little procession moved off with Leonardo and the now very vocal calf leading the way home. The poor cow, which was fast recovering her strength, was in quite a quandary. She dearly wanted to dig her horns into Leonardo yet didn't want to harm her baby. For the entire trip back to the sede we were occupied trying to separate the cow from the calf and her horns from Leonardo or his horse. It is often the horse that gets the worst of the deal. Leonardo, usually the joker of the pack, had his hands full trying to balance the calf across the saddle, as well as keeping his legs away from the cow. He had no choice but to let the horse look after himself, as he was unable to react quickly enough to manoeuvre the horse when the cow did make it past the other horses. Although the poor horse did get one butting, he also managed to kick back at the cow a few times.

It was well past bedtime before we were able to deposit mother and child in a paddock near the milking corral, unsaddle the horses and then get home for a late meal and a much-needed rest.

Trailing cattle out in the open country needs all the skill of horse and rider. There are often no fences and the cattle are not used to being told what to do or where to go. Wild cattle are understandably afraid of these strange, part humans with four legs who make scary noises and crack whips at them. From time to time it all becomes too much stress and an individual makes a break for it and heads for the nearest cover. It is important to bring the breakaway back to the herd with minimum fuss in order to prevent a stampede. The herd is halted, while some of the men go after the truant. Usually he can be flushed out and brought back without too much fuss although once in a while he needs to be lassoed and tethered until the herd can be brought near. Given a choice the steer would far prefer to be back amongst the herd.

One time a steer had been caught after a long chase and tethered by the horns to a tree. The cowboys left him there for a few minutes while they helped the others to get the herd close in the hopes of calming down the scared animal and making it easier to return him to the herd. The poor steer became so desperate during those moments that he pulled against the lasso with such a panic driven force that the horns and the tip of his skull broke off and were left tethered to the tree. The steer had somehow been able to run about a hundred yards before collapsing.

Chasing after cattle in the rough scrubland led to many surprises.

I have lost hats and shirts and even trousers through having to rush through the bushes after a steer. There are potholes and anthills as well as tree stumps hidden in the grass, any of which could cause a horse to fall. It was a constant puzzle to me how we were able to return everyday with the same number of men and horses that we had set out with. It was of course always a great joke if someone did go sprawling but there was never any laughter until it was clear that the man and his horse were unhurt. Once that was established the ribbing would be without mercy.

As the commitiva moved around the farm we were constantly inspecting fences, gates or watering places. We searched the horizon for any signs of vultures, as this could mean either a dead animal or a newborn calf. Whatever needed to be done was done then and there. We had to turn our hands to many things using either what we carried or what was available in the field. Sometimes we had fences to mend, gates to rehang or even bridges to repair. Our saddlebags had more junk in them than a woman's handbag. Someone would always have that vital little piece or wire when we needed it, a pair of pliers or a nail. Lassos and whip handles could be put to a variety of uses. Every man on the team had a razor sharp knife tucked into the back of his trousers. Whenever we found a dead steer we would try to save the skin. If the vultures had not torn it to shreds, or it had not been dead too long, the men's knives would come out from the sheathes and the precious skin would be clear of the animal in a matter of minutes, without a nick in the valuable leather. The extra leather always came in useful for lassos, whips, bridles and repairs to saddles.

Sebastiao was a good teacher. He was a tough, hard man who had been born and raised in the Pantanal region, where life was even tougher than the more leisurely parts of Mato Grosso. He showed neither fear nor sense of humour. I have seen the man jump from his horse onto a running steer and grapple him to the ground. The young members of the commitiva feared him as much as respected him and I saw them suffer from his anger more than once, sometimes with a clip across the face or a kick. I did not feel that Sebastiao relished the task of teaching yet another Ingles would-be-cowboy, nevertheless he did a good job of it and I learned a great deal from him. Being with the commitiva for days on end forced me to learn not only their ways but also their language. I had reached quite a high level of Portuguese by the time I had left Tres Barros but in Mato Grosso, with the Richardsons away for such long periods I had to speak Portuguese all the time. There is quite a difference in the Portuguese spoken in Mato Grosso to the way it is spoken in the Sao Paulo or Rio de Janeiro. Being fairly close to Paraguay there is a great deal of Spanish influence plus a variety of flavours from the often-colourful local dialect.

I never got to like Sebastiao although I respected him a great deal. There was also no great love lost between him and his team yet they too respected the man. I often sensed a tension and resentment as we rode together. Travelling the distances we had to, meant that we spent a lot of time sitting astride gently walking horses in a close bunch. Often there was light conversation and plenty of ribbing amongst the commitiva; at other times there was silence, every man apparently intensely interested in the rhythmic movement of his horse's head. Some months later I was to find out just how much the commitiva hated Sebastiao.

Gradually in the months that followed, I acquired more responsibility and so, regrettably spent less time with the commitiva.

14

ALONE IN THE WILDS OF BRAZIL

Fred soon took to the vast expanses of Mato Grosso and followed me for miles across the semi-desert, often rugged terrain of the region. There were many things to chase besides cattle, like the giant Rheas, which could always be found in an area not far from the sede. Fred had no chance of catching these huge flightless birds that could reach speeds of 40 mph. I was hard pressed to keep up with them in the jeep. Fred had no trouble chasing what the locals called the Tamandua Bandeiro, which was in fact the Giant Anteater. They have a long pointed head and a huge bushy, longhaired tail. The true Tamanduas are about half the size of the Giant Anteater. These beautiful animals can be as long as seven to eight feet, from nose to tip of tail and feed mainly on termites. They trundled along slowly enough for the playful cowboys to tease them, by holding on to the animal's tail as they ran. I called Fred off however, when he started to chase one of these funny, slow moving, cuddly creatures. If he got in front of one, he could be killed by one slash of his sharp, steel hard claws—designed to rip through the concrete-like termite hills that dotted the landscape.

One day we were riding along the edge of the forest, when a lone wolf loped along in front of us. Fred took up the chase. The rather scraggy looking wolf was twice Fred's size but took to his heels and disappeared into the trees. Fred fortunately answered my call and returned, unaware that he might just have bitten off more than he could chew.

I was always a little worried about Fred coming across a rattlesnake. If he had become too curious or disturbed a mother on a nest he could have come to a nasty end. Usually a rattlesnake stays hidden and only wants to be left alone. When there was a fire in a pasture, rattlesnakes could be seen fleeing from the flames; this was another time when you wouldn't want to make them more cross than they already were.

It was rugged, largely uncultivated country in Mato Grosso. The huge open pastures were very different to the lush greens I was used to in Tres Barros. The soil was mostly rust red and was often no more than fine sand, where little or no grass would grow. The grass that was to be found was a very coarse, tufty sort of grass. Even trees were scarce over much of the land. What trees there were, were stunted, little more than bushes. Where the land had been left alone, near rivers or in steep hillsides, the jungle could be quite thick. Once rich virgin jungle land has been cleared, it quickly turns to desert. A few large trees existed around the sede, which had obviously been carefully left for shelter.

I had to find my own way around for a lot of the time, learning my place in the business of running the fazenda by trial and error. Peter Richardson was away a lot on buying trips. He would fly up into the Pantanal area and spend several weeks farm hopping, to buy enough thin young steers to send to the company's fattening farms in the State of Sao Paulo. The Pantanal is a vast area of flat savannah. It is a good breeding area for wild herds of cattle. In the wet season it becomes almost waterlogged for months on end, so that there is a limited buying period, while the pastures and more importantly, roads are accessible. When the land gets too wet, it is difficult to trail the cattle. Once the cattle have been bought, sometimes in small numbers from different fazendas, they were assembled to make up a sizeable boiada. These boiadas, sometimes up to a thousand strong, would have to be walked for several weeks, even months before reaching Ligacao. When the boiadas arrived I would have to receive them, get them vaccinated and temporarily put to pasture. Arrangements would be made to have the cattle sent on to the Sao Paulo fattening farms by train.

Fred was my constant companion through most of my working day, always close at hand and ready to lend a hand; I only left him behind if I was going to be away for a few days.

15

A TRAIN JOURNEY TO REMEMBER

From time to time I had to travel between the three farms in Mato Grosso. If I was very lucky, my boss Peter Richardson, who besides being the cattle buyer, was also over-all manager of the three Mato Grosso farms, would be going my way and I could fly with him in the 'teko teko,' a small taxi plane, usually a Cessna like the one I had ridden in with Fred. More often than not I was left to the mercy of the narrow-gauge Brazilian railway. It started somewhere in Paraguay and crossed Mato Grosso and then continued down into the State of Sao Paulo. This is the railway line and the stations I recently revisited with Rod Paxton and Richard Turnley. They are sad reminders of their former importance to the region.

The Ligacao station was about twenty-five minutes away from the Sede by jeep. There was no telephone, so I would usually send a boy down to find out what time the next rain was expected. The timetable read 'Mondays, Wednesdays and Fridays' however, as with all timetables, it was not known for its accuracy.

My first journey was to Mutum and I planned to leave on the Wednesday train. On Tuesday afternoon I sent the sede retireiro's son, Shoo, down to the station. He returned to tell me that Monday's train was due to arrive sometime that night. After an early dinner, I threw my saddle, cape, hammock and saddle-bag into the jeep, and after a fond farewell from Fred, was driven to the station.

As the jeep disappeared into the night, I settled down for an indefinite wait for the train. A few other passengers were also waiting. Two young cowboys sang Brazilian love songs to a guitar, whilst an elderly, somewhat over dressed man sat stiffly on the only bench. The stationmaster appeared some time later to announce that Monday's train was further delayed and would probably arrive early next morning, Wednesday. There was, I knew, a shelter down by the loading corral where I could sling my hammock. I gathered my belongings and headed across the track towards the corrals, where I had spent many a night loading cattle.

"Good evening Senhor." I looked up to see the elderly man, hat raised in greeting.

"Good evening to you Senhor." I replied.

"I am a candidate for the position on the local Council representing this region; I hope that I can count on your vote."

"I am honoured Senhor, alas as a foreigner I am not entitled to vote."

The political smile vanished and he shuffled off to talk to the cowboys, who had also come in search of shelter. A few more people arrived, as the evening wore on, and someone eventually lit a fire, bringing a little cheer to the cold night air. I lay in my hammock listening to the sounds of Brazilian music, interspersed with some impassioned political oratory from the would-be councillor, before drifting off to sleep.

When I awoke there was a dull blue light, just enough to make out the crouched figure of one of the cowboys, intent on re-lighting the fire.

"Any news of the train, Amigo?" I called out.

"No Senhor, but you need not worry, the stationmaster will call us." He fanned the small flame for a few moments.

"Would you like some Matte?"

"I would be most grateful." I lay there watching as the fire began to brighten the little shelter. The flames were now lapping the small tin of water, suspended above it. Wrapping my cape around me, I squatted down in front of the fire as other silent forms joined us. When the water boiled, the Matte gourd was filled with the rather bitter herbal tea, and passed around. Each person took a mouthful, through the hollowed silver drinking spoon, warming his hands around the gourd for a moment, before passing it on or passing it back for more hot water. I felt the strong, sharp yet not unpleasant taste penetrating my system, clearing my brain, and leaving me with a contented glow; ready to face the day. Frequent drinkers could get quite addicted to the Matte.

The cold dawn soon began to turn into another hot, dry Mato Grosso day. The young peons stripped off and plunged into the little stream; I followed suit. The first plunge into the clear running water was breath-catchingly cold but after a moment I was able to relax and let the farmyard smells of the night wash down the stream.

It was well into the morning before the stationmaster proudly announced that the Monday train would be arriving shortly; that would be around midday on Wednesday. I mentioned that the timetable was not always accurate.

"Would you send a message down the line to Agua Clara for me?" I asked the stationmaster. "Address it to Senhor Batista in Fazenda Mutum, to tell him I am on this train."

"Do not worry, Senhor, I will do it as soon as the train leaves."

Black ugly smoke heralded the arrival of the iron horse, followed by the invasive clanging and wheezing of a train losing speed. The quiet little station, barely more than a platform in the middle of the desert, was suddenly all business. Doors opened, people bustled about, the stationmaster shouting orders, the train driver making demands, and the guard looking important. Passengers alighted from the train, mostly to stretch their legs.

"All aboard." The whistle blew and the bell clanged. With a hissing and a squealing, the train laboriously pulled out of the station. The politician found another captive audience and was soon launching into his now all too familiar political spiel. I settled back to let sleep help shorten the journey.

Our first stop was another cattle loading station, with just a cluster of simple houses nearby. A few people waited on the platform to board the train, amongst them I noticed one man wearing a cape, with his broad hat pulled down. He was leaning motionless against the wall and did not stir even as the people started to board the train.

The politician obviously saw no new votes in the joining passengers, or was just plain out of political rhetoric, and had fallen asleep with his head against the carriage window. Once again the whistle blew; the train shuddered and ground its way forward. As the train began to edge along the platform, the man in the cape ambled casually across the platform. When the sleeping politician drew abreast of him, he produced a large 45 from beneath his cape and fired at point blank range. The bullet made a neat hole through the window and the politician's head, ricocheted off the carriage ceiling, and fell, spent, onto the lap of a woman, sitting across the aisle. I glanced quickly at the receding platform but it was deserted.

At first there was a stunned, unbelieving silence and then the woman began to scream. The politician campaigned no more. He remained as if still sleeping but the rhythm of the train caused him to slowly arch forward, leaving a crescent of blood on the window, before slumping to the floor.

The next stop was Ribas do Rio Pardo. The would-be councillor was removed quietly from the train. The local storekeeper-cum-sheriff asked a few questions and then the train continued on its way.

As the train pulled into the next station we were transported into fairyland. The platform was ablaze with lights, and people were dancing. We were greeted by waving arms and smiling faces, as arms grabbed the doors and people made us welcome. Sleeping passengers awoke and stared in disbelief, rubbing their eyes and expecting all the madness to be just a dream.

"Come Senhor, drink to my daughter's wedding." A merry little man said, as he grabbed my hand.

Another hand appeared from somewhere and thrust a glass full of neat Pinga into mine.

"You are Ingles? No?" My host was obviously not as drunk as I had thought.

"Yes, Senhor I am. I congratulate you on your daughter's marriage."

"Come! You must meet the couple." He led me into the station office.

Two rather bewildered, almost frightened, children sat in their brand-new clothes and shyly acknowledged my compliments. Neither could have been more than fourteen years old and I would have put the girl nearer twelve.

I raised my glass to the couple and took a mouthful of neat Pinga. I felt my mucosa shrivel, as the distilled sugar started its journey. The top of my head blew off and the room was filled with stars. I braced my knees and held a smile, waiting for the room to stop spinning, before walking stiff legged out to the platform.

"Come dance with a lonely girl." A well-fed matron, with alternate teeth missing, grabbed my hand and started to gyrate along the platform. The lights became a blur. I remember drinking a toast to the bride's father, the groom's father, the groom's mother and probably the bride's mother. Somehow the festivity all got rolled into one crazy kaleidoscope, punctuated by lights, music and smiling, buxom, often toothless matrons, all wanting to dance with the Ingles. I am not sure however I seem to remember dancing with the engine driver, at one point.

Eventually somebody decided that the train should continue on its journey, and so after a few rounds of drinks for the rail, we somehow found our way back to our respective places. The train's whistle blew long and loud, and the stationmaster, not to be outdone, blew his until his face became apoplectic. Complete strangers bade fond loving farewells to complete strangers, promising to write although forgetting to tell them their names, let-alone addresses. The cheering and waving reached a climax, as the train pulled, even more jerkily than usual, out of the station.

An hour or so along the narrow track, we pulled into another small station, and there we stayed. The driver had been taken mysteriously ill and needed some rest. I decided to walk off my own screaming hangover as well as find some breakfast.

For a few cruzeiros, I was served with rice and beans, a little ground mandioca, some sickly sweet dolce de leite and of course, black coffee. It was just another cattle loading station. My walk took me down to the corral, where a group of cowboys were herding a boiada into the corral to await the arrival of a train later that night. I was able to sit back and watch other people doing what I usually did.

I finally arrived at my destination, the small town of Agua Clara, more of a village by most comparisons. The few houses were in a row, parallel to the railway. The narrow street, that separated the station from the town, was no more than an earth track, dusty in the dry season and like a mud pond in the wet.

"Did you receive my message?" I asked the stationmaster.

"Si Senhor, it is here." He waved a sheet of paper.

"Did you inform Senhor Batista?"

"Not yet Senhor, I shall do that now." He smiled proudly and went off towards the town.

It was my first trip to Agua Clara, so I did not know the way yet more importantly I did not even have a horse. I would have to wait for Batista to send someone. I resigned myself to a long wait, slung my hammock and settled down for a nap.

"Senhor Bruce," I woke to a persistent prodding, to find a young boy's face a few inches from mine.

"Yes. Who are you?" I asked sleepily.

"I am Francisco, son of Senhor Batista. He has sent me to take you to the fazenda." He indicated two horses waiting nearby. It turned out that young Francisco had spent the night with an aunt who lived in the village, waiting for me to arrive. A few minutes later I was obediently following little bare-foot Francisco along the main street of Aqua Clara for the eight-mile ride to the sede of Mutum, the company's largest property in Brazil. When the Vesteys had first purchased it, it was said to be as big as Britain up to the Wash. Some sections of it were sold off later though it still remained a huge area of land. Herds of cattle that were rounded up, from time to time, often contained full-grown cows and bulls that had never been branded, and so had never seen man before. It was an amazing experience to ride the virtually wild country, where there were no fences except close to the retiros. The land was richer and the greenery more lush than ours in Ligacao. Riding through the remnants of a once dense jungle, interspersed by open areas, was like a trip through a natural history museum. The air as we rode under a group of trees, could suddenly become a kaleidoscope of sound and colour as parrots, macaws or cockatoos took to the air in protest to our presence.

Batista, the Brazilian manager, greeted me when I arrived and apologized for not having met me at the station but having no telephone he had been unable to get news of the train's progress and approach. He had sent young Francisco to stay with his aunt, Batista's wife's sister, once he had heard that I was expected. It was no great chore, as Francisco enjoyed a few days with his nephews as well as the break from farm routine in the local town, hamlet would be a better word. After lunch we started to do some of the counting around the sede. We counted the horses, mules and the milk cattle and then started the more tedious business of counting all the goods and chattels of the farm. The furniture in the Manager's house was simple enough, as well as the larger items, like the generator for the electricity and the heavy farm implements; we even had to account for every spade, or pick, and hoe. Even buckets had to be accounted for. Any of the tools that had been broken, or become useless since the last count were kept, so that they could be officially written off at this time. It was all rather tedious yet as we went from retiro to retiro, I was able to get some idea of the size of the property.

We drove all one morning to get to the furthest retiro and yet there was a great deal of land beyond that, which had been left to its own devices and remained unfenced. The cost of fencing such a vast boundary would have been enormous but our boundary met only more arid, semi-jungle and in some areas virgin jungle. The retiro was no more than a very primitive homestead where a family of bugries, half Indians, lived in total isolation. Their clothes were threadbare and the house little more than a shelter, made of logs and mud. The whole family turned out to greet us with all the excitement of a festive occasion. Two elder boys helped their father and a teenage daughter helped her mother with the house and looking after four younger children. In spite of their obvious hard and simple life they struck me as being a very happy group. The location itself was beautiful, nestled in between two small jungle hills, with a stream running close to the house. Before I left the whole group of children dragged me down to the stream, where we spent a while skinny-dipping in the clear sparkling stream water.

I spent the nights back at the sede in the guesthouse, which was separate from the manager's house; conveniently located next to the office and storeroom. It was a plain room, with the minimum of furniture yet it was clean and quite acceptable. I ate with the family and found them to be very pleasant people who ran the farm without any feeling of superiority over the other people on it. I was most impressed one evening during dinner, when Batista mentioned that one of the commitiva was away for the night helping on another retiro. His wife noted that the man's wife would be alone that night, and that she was always nervous of sleeping in the house alone. It was decided that the ever-willing Francisco would go over and spend the night with the cowboy's wife.

On this my first trip to Mutum, I was taken for a grand tour and loved every minute of it. We had to count every thing on every retiro, so we had to cover them all, spending a day sometimes just to cover one retiro and the cattle belonging to it.

We were just about to set out one morning for another retiro, when we heard the sound of an approaching aircraft and moments later saw a Cessna overhead. It circled twice and then came in to land. It was Peter Richardson making a surprise visit. It had been decided that some of the Mutum steers should be included in the next trainload of cattle, bound for the fattening farms in the State of Sao Paulo. Peter needed a few hundred to make up the numbers. There had been a bad outbreak of foot and mouth disease in one of the boiadas that he had bought, and so they were quite short. Half an hour later, having made the arrangements for the cattle to be rounded up the next day, Peter was racing down the runway once more, leaving us to continue our day's counting a little behind schedule.

During the following day we rounded up the cattle for shipping and that evening I joined the commitiva as we herded them to the station. I had finished my counting so after loading the cattle, I hung up my hammock along with the team from Mutum and slept till dawn. I bade the team, which included the tireless Francisco, a fond farewell and stayed at the station to wait for the next passenger train through to return to Ligacao.

For the entire time I had been away, Fred had moped around the house, not wanting to eat. My housekeeper was quite worried and did not know what to do. She had no idea when I would return and so could not have done anything to indicate my imminent return although Fred somehow knew. The day before I returned, Fred started to eat and kept going out into the garden to look for me. On the day of my arrival, he was getting quite agitated and excited. Finally he left the garden and went to the sede. When I arrived at the station, I borrowed a horse from the stationmaster and rode the fairly short distance home. As I entered the last gate before the sede, who should be waiting, ears erect, tail wagging but my ever-faithful Fred. He turned, and proudly escorted me back to the sede, barking to make sure everyone knew that his master was back and that all was well with the world.

Then
Main Street, Ribas do Rio Pardo

Now
Ribas do Rio Pardo today, definitely the wrong side of the track.

16

A CUSTOM MADE LASSO

The commitiva made their own lassos, so there was always a great deal of interest in the choice of cow, or steer, to be killed each week for consumption by the farm personnel. The quality of a man's lasso along with his boots and hat were his badges of rank and status whether real or fantasy; he would sacrifice his children's food or clothing in order to be able to have the full regalia of a Brazilian cowboy.

It was usually my job to select the animal for the butcher's knife. Besides the obvious need for an animal that was healthy looking and reasonably well stocked with meat, it was also necessary to find an animal with good skin. Usually the animals that we selected were cows that had stopped producing milk in an acceptable quantity, or did not produce calves. The Warble fly was a problem but not as serious as it had been on Tres Barros. Most of the cattle in Mato Grosso were the lighter coloured Nelore, one of the strains of the Indian humped cattle known as Zebu, but there were always a few dark brown, red or black, from the Gyr or Indo Brazilian strains, which would be often dotted with Warble scars. On the whole the Zebu strains were much more parasite resistant than the European crosses; one of the reasons was that they have muscles under the skin with which they can twitch and so ward off flies and ticks. Other possible flaws could include bad scars, or badly placed brand marks. Unless the farm needed them the skins were sold to the cowboys, for a very nominal sum; there was some system of rote amongst the farm workers, so a man might have to wait for a while before his turn came up. All the cowboys, both breeding and commitiva, were keen to get their turn; so that when their turn did come up they were very anxious to see what animal was chosen. Whether they were going to use the leather for lasso or other purposes they wanted a skin that was clear of flaws.

There were of course the occasional deaths in the field, which would add to the number of skins available although sadly the vultures often ruined them before we were able to find the animal and remove the skin. Sometimes there were cows that had to be killed for consumption in spite of their damaged hide; in which case the farm took the skin and let the next in line wait for the next time.

I decided to get one of the men to make a lasso for me. When we next killed one from the herd for meat, I went out with the man who was going to make my lasso. Quite unabashedly, we selected the animal strictly according to the skin quality; luckily the meat was quite good as well. Having selected our skin, and incidentally meat, we returned to the sede to deliver her to the man with the knife. The method of killing out on the farm was not without its morbid side. The poor animal was tied, with its head against a thick pole, in a clean grassy area outside the corral. This was to avoid the dust of the corral contaminating the meat. One man would bind the hind legs and then hold the tail. The head was held close to the pole by lasso, with the tension held by another man. The butcher waits for the animal to calm a little, and then with a thrust of the razor sharp knife he severs the Carotid artery. At first the animal reacts from the pain though only momentarily. Then as the arterial blood is being pumped through the wound, the cow quickly shows signs of weakening, the eyes become dull, and then as she falls the lasso is released. The man on the tail pulls the now lifeless animal so that she falls clear of the pole and the blood. The skin is cut clear though left beneath the body, to act as a sterile base on which to section the carcass. I could never quite get used to the idea of carrying my meat home, while it was still twitching.

The skin was now stretched, salted, and then left in the sun for several days to really dry out. Once that had happened, four squares were cut in the hide, as large as the hide would allow. The hair was shaved off and then the squares were soaked in water for twenty-four hours, to make them soft. Now came the delicate task of cutting a continuous coil of hide, less than a centimetre wide in each of the squares; the corners were of course rounded off before the cutting began. The four strips of hide were then soaked for a further twenty-four hours, tied at one end and allowed to stretch to their full length in the stream below the corral. In this way the strands began to form as straight lengths of leather. Drying and stretching the strands between posts completed the process. The last little detail, before the strand was ready, was the laborious job of scraping away all the excess loose fibres on the under side of the hide. Now the platting could begin. It was done with loving care, so that the lasso was of even thickness throughout, with no lumps or kinks. The final job was to secure the end ring, which must be large enough to allow plenty of room for the lasso to pass through. The ring should be brass or stainless steel, so as not to rust. The joint in the ring must by flawless, so that no sharp edges cut into the leather of the lasso.

Once the lasso was complete, a period of working out and breaking in must be done, so as to stretch the lasso and tighten the weave. I spent many hours practising, so as to be able to do my treasured new lasso justice. The cowboy who made the lasso for me already had a good lasso and had been happy to use his turn for a little profit.

It is quite a common sight to see the cowboys returning from the field, with their lassos stretching their lengths behind the horses. This was to take out all the kinks and allow the lasso to stretch. I had been using a series of borrowed lassos since my Tres Barros days but this one was mine; made for me and very personal and very special.

17

SEBASTIAO, A GRISSLY DISCOVERY

It was to have been just a normal routine inspection. I called Sebastiao in on the Monday morning and told him to take the commitiva out to inspect the Pontal and Cachoeira sections. This would take a few days, as they would have to do some branding when they found cattle that escaped the hot iron in the past. Sometimes cattle were sick or had been injured and would require some crude treatment out in the field. These two sections were vast open areas of sandy scrub out at the furthest part of the fazenda.

"There's been no rain out there for months; God knows what they are finding to eat." I remarked.

"They'll find something, even if it is bark from the trees." Sebastiao rarely looked at me when he spoke, but seemed to address his remarks to someone on the far horizon. "It's lack of water that will kill them. If the river dries up we're in real trouble.

"Try to get a count if you can." I asked, realising as I did so, that I was asking the impossible, it was a vast area, and the cattle would be spread out in search of food.

"We will do what we can, Senhor."

The commitiva assembled an hour or so later with the usual supplies of rice and beans, some dried meat, mandioca and of course, the Brazilian's life blood, coffee and the fine powdery sugar. With their saddlebags bulging and saddles draped with hammocks, capes and lassos, they were ready for the trip. They all had guns and would try to shoot some wild game to alternate their diet. Sometimes it would be a wild pig, an armadillo, or a bird of some sort. Even in those days the local people did not like to kill the wildlife except out of necessity; it was not regarded as a sport except by some townspeople who sometimes asked permission to shoot on our land. Permission was not granted and their presence was not welcome.

"I am going out part of the way, so I'll ride with you," I said.

We headed out, fording the almost dry stream below the sede, a reminder of the long drought. I rode ahead with Sebastiao, discussing a few matters of concern. I never felt comfortable talking with the capitaz; he sat erect, face hard and expressionless. Sebastiao's lined and tanned face, sheltered by a black wide brimmed hat pulled well down on to his head, remained facing the way we were going. Often my questions or comments were greeted by long silent pauses and then the curtest of answers. The men of the commitiva rode behind us in unusual silence.

"Heh Idimur! How do like being with the commitiva?" I turned in my saddle to ask the boy. He was the son of the breeding capitaz and had yearned to break with tradition and leave the rather sheltered world of the small milk and breeding retiro and join the commitiva. I had finally persuaded his father to let him break away from the family, and be the first of his many sons to work the range.

"It's all right Patron." was the sullen reply. I was usually only addressed as Patron by a complete stranger, who was going out of his way to show respect. The men knew me as Senhor Bruce. I sensed something was wrong. Usually when the commitiva cowboys were riding together, they were talking and joking. Sometimes they would ride a little behind one cowboy, and wait until he was almost asleep on his horse, then with a quick crack of the whip just beneath the horse's tail, they would try to unseat him. It was very seldom that the ruse worked although it caused great amusement amongst the cowboys.

I made a few more attempts to draw them out but was greeted with a sulky silence. At the time I thought nothing of it. I naturally took it that the commitiva had had some slight disagreement with Sebastiao, or perhaps between themselves. We stopped for a while to let the horses drink at a small stream called Agua Limpa, meaning 'clean water'. Legend has it that once you have tasted water from the stream, you will always return. I left the commitiva after we had rested, and went to rendezvous with a strange and colourful couple, who were our fence contractors. I rode for a further half an hour before a little column of smoke lead me to their campsite. The smell of coffee brewing over an open fire was a welcome bonus.

"Bon Dia Senhor, come and join us for a caffezino." Oswaldo, and his rugged little wife, greeted me. I dismounted to join them in a mug of the brew. It was powerful stuff, and required a lot of sugar to take away the sting but it was good. I had last seen Oswaldo and his wife when they had come in for stores a month before. They had been working on building a new fence for three months already, living where they worked, in a remote corner of the farm. We had decided to divide one huge pasture into two. The fence was several miles long, crossing some pretty dense scrubland. This tough pair had had to clear a strip of land twenty feet wide and then build a five-strand wire fence. Oswaldo had sent a message with a passing rider, to say that one section of the fence was complete. We had agreed to pay him at various intervals once the section of fence has been inspected and counted.

"Let's start the count." I said, after finishing my coffee.

"Here is the figure, you can take my word." Oswaldo pushed a piece of paper in front of me with a column of rather crude, almost childlike, figures.

"I am sure your figures are right Senhor but you know the rules, I must count them." Fence counting is not a very exciting job. One has to ride along the entire length of a fence counting the posts, making two or three different counts. There are the normal posts, the one in twenty stronger posts and the corner or gateposts that have to be stronger and sunk a lot deeper, they also have diagonal support posts to give them the extra strength they need. The contractors get paid according to the numbers of posts, with a different price for the three types. This was just a straight fence so that there were no corners although one gate connected the two halves of the original pasture.

I got home at about ten that night, tired from a day in the saddle and grateful for a meal, although now cold left for me by my housekeeper, who lived down near the station and so had to walk for half an hour to get home.

The week went by as normal. I saw nothing of the commitiva and did not expect to. I did not ride out to see them this time, as I sometimes did. There was quite a lot to do in the sede, what with incoming cattle for branding, vaccinating and despatching to the fattening farms in the south. There was also the normal fieldwork. With most of the commitiva away, I was needed as an extra hand, especially in rounding up and trailing the cattle. I was very busy.

On Sunday evening, an hour or so before dark, I wandered down to the milking shed, to have a look at one of the calves that had been a little sick. The little fellow had had a touch of diarrhoea at early milking and the retireiro had mentioned it to me. He seemed to be better when I got there but I checked him out anyway. I had not been there for more than ten minutes, before I saw the commitiva arriving at the crossing point of the river. I walked across to the main corral to see Sebastiao and ask him how he got on, only to find that he was not with the others.

"Where is Sebastiao?" I enquired.

"He was following some way back, and may be an hour or so arriving," came the rather sulky reply. It was fairly late already, so I decided not to wait for him and headed back to the house.

At early morning muster the next day, I looked again for Sebastiao but did not see him. The men said that he had not returned yet, which did not cause me any alarm. I knew Sebastiao well: he would have a good reason for not getting back. The commitiva would have the day off, as they had been away all week, and worked on Sunday, so there was no need for Sebastiao to be there.

By the following day, I was perhaps a little annoyed by Sebastiao's non-return, as I had some cattle that had to be taken out to pasture. Without his report I could not decide where to send them. It was Wednesday before I decided that something must have gone wrong. I told the commitiva to stock up again and go out to look for their capitaz. I had a gut feeling that something was seriously wrong. I therefore decided, at the last minute, to go along as well. I saddled up and, taking a hammock and some food, led the commitiva out towards Pontal.

We didn't arrive at Pontal until nearly nightfall, having made several detours on the way, to make sure that he had not met with an accident on the way back. The cowboys had been very vague about the exact time they had last seen Sebastiao, so I had nothing to go on at all. We made camp that evening, spending a very silent night. Food was cooked and passed around, without a word being spoken by anyone. I tried without success to break through and get some co-operation but failed.

The next morning we were up before dawn and in the saddle as the sun was rising. I took up position in the centre. It was a long ride that day, through the bushy country, forcing our way through the undergrowth, all the time searching for a trace of Sebastiao, or his horse. Nightfall came once more. Again we camped and passed the night in silence. Those gut feelings returned the following day, as I sent the cowboys off in another sweep.

"I'll meet you at the far fence." I called as we separated. We had visited all the camping places regularly used by the commitiva, except for one, which was down near the river, at the far end of a valley. I decided to go there myself. I had had the feeling the previous day that I was being steered away from that area. I waited until the cowboys were over the ridge, and then headed for the river.

As I came out of the trees, about a half-mile away from the camp, I found my path blocked by the entire commitiva, statue-like; their eyes fixed menacingly on mine.

"You don't need to go down there, Senhor." It was Claudio, a tall soft-spoken man, with a face carved from granite. "We have been to the river, there is nothing there."

I edged my horse on past the men and came to the brow of a hill. That was when I saw the vultures. Some were flying around but most were sitting in the trees. Although this could have meant only that there was a dead or dying steer, or even some wild animal, I somehow felt that the search was over. With my heart pounding in my breast, and the blood draining from my face, I urged my already tired horse down the hill. As I neared the campsite, I saw what I had half expected to see. The vultures were crowded round the simple thatch shelter, which had been used by the commitiva for camping. Tethered to the shelter was a horse, still saddled with Sebastiao's saddle, his head lowered almost to the ground, suffering from lack of water and food. I cannot imagine how he had lasted that long.

My eyes remained fixed on the horse, as I rode up, dreading the sight I was bound to find. I had seen a dead man before but he had died of illness and had lain as in sleep with a peaceful expression on his face; this was different. Sebastiao, it could only be he, lay grotesque and horrible. He was without eyes and with his entrails open to the air—a vulture's delicacy. I turned away and averting my eyes from the sight. I busied myself with unsaddling the half-dead horse. I led him down to the river to drink, making sure that he did not drink too much at first. As I stood there while the poor animal drank from the barely moving stream, I thought of happier times when I had camped here. The river had been full then. A waterfall that was now reduced to a trickle had made a great place to bathe at the end of a day in the field. I let the poor animal loose to find some food.

Even while my back had been turned the vultures had returned for more pickings. Already filled to the point of bursting, some could hardly walk, yet they still would not leave the man alone. Struck with a sudden frenzy, I ran towards them, cracking my whip and screaming at them, venting my fury and disgust at the whole affair. After a while I steeled myself to look at Sebastiao, determinedly fighting my gag reflex, I edged closer to try to find out how he had died. I turned the poor man onto his face and found a short bloody tear in his shirt and a knife wound deep between his ribs, about an inch and a half wide.

A movement behind me made me turn. The men, who I had momentarily forgotten, were gathered silently, menacingly, a few feet away. The full impact of my position hit me, as a cold rivulet of sweat trickled down my spine. I was alone, unarmed, in the depths of the Mato Grosso, facing four armed men; knowing that one of them had killed Sebastiao, whose body lay at my feet.

"He must have had a heart attack." I said, as convincingly as I could. "Joao, get his cape and cover him," I ordered, as matter-of-factly as my quivering vocal chords could manage.

There was a deathly silence as I locked eyes on Joao. I then looked from one to the other, only to be met by a cold menacing stare. After what seemed like hours, Joao dismounted and fetched Sabastiao's cape from his saddle. The tension eased as the grotesque spectre disappeared beneath the cape. Suddenly they all dismounted and busied themselves with the job at hand.

"You are right Senhor; it must have been a heart attack."

I felt my own tension that I had not been consciously aware of, drain out of me to the point where I felt my knees buckle. I caught myself just before I started to fall and returned to the job at hand.

The cowboys at least pretended to believe what I had said. We piled the saddle and the hammock on top of the cape and then some rocks to keep away the vultures. After checking on the horse, to make sure that he had found some grass—there was luckily some near the water's edge—we started home at a more leisurely pace. It was a very awkward ride home, there was some attempt at conversation but mostly we kept to our thoughts. I felt sure that one of the commitiva had delivered the fatal wound but I was in no position to say so. They in turn must have realized that I suspected them. It was well after dark before we reached home, tired, both physically and emotionally. We separated without a word, and went to our own houses for rest.

I did not sleep well that night, despite my fatigue. The awful spectre kept returning. I found it hard to grasp that the almost childlike cowboys, with whom I had so often joked and played, had killed their leader and left him and his horse to the vultures.

The next morning I sent two men out to Pontal, with a cart to bring back the body. I questioned the men from the commitiva about what had happened but they said nothing. Peter was away on a buying trip and I realized there was no point sending for the police, they never left the town area. I knew that I was up against a wall. These cowboys would never let each other down, so we had to just bury the body, notify the officials in Campo Grande that there had been an accidental death, and try to carry on as if nothing had happened.

It was several months before I finally heard the story, which eased my mind a little about the whole thing. I had always known that Sebastiao was a hard man yet it was not until after his death that I realized that he was also a very cruel one. Sebastiao had apparently taken a dislike to Idimur, who had just joined the comitiva from the breeding section. He had made life unbearable for him. He would always give him the heavy and unpleasant jobs to do. The cowboys went along with him to start with, they had all had it rough at the beginning and it was good to break the lad in right from the start. The cruelty did not stop at just making it tough. On the Monday morning before going out to Pontal, Sebastiao had found an excuse to punch the boy several times, for little or no reason. The cowboys had not taken this kindly; it was this that had caused the silence on the way out.

It seems that this cruelty had gone on during the week; finally down at the river camp, the boy had been slow saddling Sebastiao's horse, which was not his job at all. Sebastiao had struck him with his whip. One of the older cowboys, I was never able to find out which, had drawn his knife and stabbed Sebastiao in the back.

For a time I hated the cowboys for what they had done, until I heard the true story. I started to get to know them better over the months that followed, and couldn't have asked for a more loyal and willing group of men. The horse was found later, having spent some time in the pasture eating, drinking and taking life quietly. A few days of much needed rain had made life easier for him. I took the horse over as one of my own string and grew very fond of him.

By my English standards law by the gun did not sit comfortably, nevertheless it was the way the country people lived. Their justice was harsh though usually just. I am sure that I had not been in any real danger, that day, down at the campsite. I was unarmed and they knew that. I had been given some very good advice, shortly after arriving in Mato Grosso. My boss Peter Richardson had said, "Remember that during your dealing with the men, you may often get angry or frustrated. If you are wearing a gun, and you wave your arms around in anger, the movement may be misinterpreted as going for your gun. The man who feels threatened by that movement will instinctively go for his own gun, before you can go for yours. If you have no gun and they know that, then you can wave your arms around, rant and rave without fear of being shot at.

The only times I did carry a gun, was when I had to carry large quantities of money. This I had to do every time we loaded cattle onto a train. The stationmaster would only take cash. There was only one time when I actually drew my gun, and would have used it if it had become necessary. I was alone in the jeep, off the farm, on a narrow track in the semi jungle. The track was sandy and difficult to negotiate. The only way to keep going was to keep a constant speed. Corners were all right as long as you just kept going and bounced off the side of the ruts. I was at the top of a slight hill, amongst the trees. As I crested the hill, I became aware of three cowboys, on horseback, straddling the road in the valley at the bottom of the hill. As I approached, they waved, indicating that they wanted me to stop. I was, as I have said, alone, carrying a lot of money. At the point where the men were standing, at the bottom of the hill, the sand is always deeper and usually very powdery. If I were to stop, or even slow down, my wheels would start to spin in the fine sand and I could be stranded. I had no idea what the men wanted. Reaching down, I found my Mauser and drew it out. Driving with one hand on the wheel, I pointed my gun with the other. In a spray of dust, I sped past the three men. I nervously kept an eye on the mirror, as I climbed the next hill as fast as my jeep would take me. The men had pulled away just in time and were staring at me as I sped away, obviously a little taken aback but to my great relief they did not start shooting.

I have no idea what they may have wanted. It is possible that they just wanted a light for a cigarette, or to ask for directions. But then again, they could have known that I would be driving along that route, with a fortune, for them, in cash and the spot they had chosen was ideal for a hold-up; no witnesses and deep powdery sand to bog me down in.

On the way to the horse race.

18

THE HORSE RACE

"Bon Dia Senhor Bruce." Rodrigues, the Ligacao stationmaster excitedly greeted me. "Come and have a drink with my while you wait for the train."

After the many hours I had spent at his station, Rodrigues and I had developed quite a friendship. I often had to accept his hospitality, which consisted of pinga in large quantities. I usually managed to keep the amount down with the excuse that I would have to go and count cattle soon and I needed both eyes to face in the same direction.

"You must drink to my horse." Rodrigues declared as we sat in his small living room.

"Why? What did he do?" I asked.

"She," he corrected me. "She has been challenged to a race."

There were no racecourses, or regular meets of any nature, however from time to time a man who was rather proud of his horse, would let it be known that he was open for challenge. He would talk his horse up a storm and show off its paces to any possible contender. The word soon gets around and eventually somebody takes up the challenge; then the punters would start to lay the odds between the two horses. The prospect of a race challenge causes considerable excitement and speculation in an ever-increasing circle on influence. It becomes the topic of conversation for weeks before the actual race date is even arranged. It is also just as much a topic for a long time after the race is over, causing hero status for the winner and humiliation for the loser.

"You must come and give me support," Rodrigues insisted.

The race day was scheduled for a Sunday, so that the maximum number of people could get there. Having promised Rodrigues to be there, I set out early on the morning of the race. The racetrack was on one of the neighbouring farms, beyond the far border of Ligacao. It was some fair distance even by jeep, and I knew that many people would be journeying from even further-a-field by horse-back; so it would be an all day affair for most and a two day affair for many.

Having driven across Ligacao and then through some rough and unfamiliar territory, I arrived at the farmhouse. I had invited a couple of the commitiva, mainly because I did not want to get lost. It was always safer to have some extra people along where the route could go through some pretty rugged territory and to have an armed escort gave me a little reassurance. There was no clear track once we had left Ligacao, not that the Ligacao tracks were all that smooth but at least one of the commitiva seemed to know where we were going. Well he said he did although there seemed to be a lot of heated discussion each time we had to make a direction call. Except for one episode where one wheel sank into powdery sand, we made quite good time and found our destination.

The fazenda was a fairly small, at least by Mato Grosso standards, privately owned cattle ranch. Usually these smallholdings breed their own cattle and sell off steers for income. We pulled in to a very small, rustic sede scattered with discarded machinery, timber and livestock. A corral that looked as if it could use some new boards and a ramshackle cluster of sheds made up the rest of the business area. The simple yet surprisingly picturesque farmhouse nestled comfortably at the foot of a small hill. The centre area of the sede was already filled to capacity with people, horses and a few vehicles. I nosed my jeep as close as I could get to an old shade tree that was already home to a number of horses and a pick-up. Some of the people had clearly been there for a while, drinking the farmer's pinga and beer and were already in great spirits. The stationmaster hurried over to greet me and show me off to the assembled crowd, none of whom I had met before but they all greeted me as if I was kin. A large glass of local beer was placed in my hand, followed by some delicious roasted pork that had been cooked on a spit over an open fire. Rice, beans and mandioca soon filled my plate as I settle down for a pre-race luncheon.

The race was to start at three, so at about two, people started to make their way towards the racetrack. It was a fair walk up a narrow pathway for those of us who had come by vehicle, made a lot more difficult by the our elevated blood alcohol level although no trouble for the horsemen, as at least the horses were sober. The racetrack, which was in fact a simple emergency airstrip, was a thin strip of closely mown grass that ran along the ridge of the hill, probably no more than a quarter of a mile in length. There was just enough room for two horses to run, or a small plane to land. It was a beautiful clear day with a rich blue sky, speckled only with occasional tiny cotton ball clouds. Visibility was so clear you could see forever; the horizon was as clearly defined as the nearby trees. The hill itself was a little higher than most in the area, which was not saying very much, granting us a clear view of the rolling countryside for miles around. The gentle breeze brought with it more oven-hot air to replace the old. It was the dry season and I could see scattered signs of grass fires, some intentional but most probably spontaneous. The smoke from these fires could be seen coiling up into the sky, each one eventually forming its own cloud high in the sky. I often theorized that each of one of the small cumulus clouds, that were so typical in the interior, marked a bush or grass fire somewhere in Brazil.

A few of the cattlemen were testing the track as well as their own horses, to the cheers and jeers of the now quite considerable crowd. The noisiest group was made up of the younger ones, who had found a huge old figueiro tree, off to the side, near the end of the course that had a birds-eye view of the entire track. The kids and a few adults had climbed into its branches for a grandstand view as well as just for the fun of it.

The last minute betting was taking placed. I saw some of my own men betting as much as a months salary; I could not help thinking about the poor wives and children, who depended on that money for food and clothing. It was a male dominant society and the men had little regard for the welfare of their wives and children. The family was supposed to make do on what was left over, after the husband had spent his money on himself and on finery for his horse. In his eyes he had to look good, even if his children ran around in rags and his wife made do with one dress, and of course he had to spend money on liquor and gambling.

The race officials stepped forward, resplendent in the very finest hat, boots and jangling spurs; probably bought specially for the occasion. After a little preliminary officiating, gesticulating and posturing, the two competing horses were brought forward. Both contestants were fillies between two and three years old. The horse I had come to see was a beautiful roan, with a shining coat covering a very trim and healthy looking body; she was no farm working horse. The challenger was an equally well looked after, jet-black filly who was clearly excited and raring to go.

I was naturally a little biased towards the stationmaster's filly so I wagered a few cruzeiros on the nag, just to make things a little more interesting.

The two horses and the starter trotted down towards the far end of the track. The two jockeys edged their mounts towards the starting line and almost immediately the flag was dropped. Eight eager hooves tore at the turf as they sprang forward, accelerating with every stride. The black filly had a fraction better start and held the lead to the wire.

I was about ready to make my way back down the hill towards the jeep, mourning the loss of some hard earned cash, when someone explained that it was to be the best of three. So with my cruzeiros still riding, I waited to see what happened in the next race. With only a few minutes of rest, the horses were called forward again and away they went in a cloud of dust. The challenger seemed to be ahead again at the start but the stationmaster's filly drew up and in the final few yards spurted ahead, to pass the post by a clear neck. Now excitement was running high. The horses were given fifteen minutes to rest, so people had time to place their last bets. The figueiro tree was getting top heavy with the grandstand viewers, and most of the other spectators were using the tree for shelter. The last race was duly called. The horses were as excited as the crowd, bristling with energy, heads tossing and tails swishing. Two false starts added to the already stimulated atmosphere. The third start was good and the roan filly rocketed down the runway, to leave no doubt as to which horse was the winner.

The grandstand shook with delight, and the men on the ground showed their feelings, either delight or frustration, in the customary way, by firing their guns into the air. Unfortunately the bullets had to pass through the tree before reaching the air. It looked like a hunting man's dream, for every shot that was fired, at least two bodies dropped to the ground. Miraculously nobody was hurt that day although it sure was a hell of a way to clear the grandstand. I couldn't help but wonder where those bullets came down

Having received my winnings—not enough to retire on—I rounded up my passengers and headed down to the jeep for long and tortuous road home. I declined the invitations to continue the festivities back at the farmhouse; it was approaching evening and we still had quite a long way to go.

I had enjoyed the diversion and the company of the two lads from the commitiva, they were good company as well as being very useful whenever we came to one of the many gates that needed to be opened and closed along the way. Most importantly I got the feeling that they accepted me almost as one of them; my Portuguese was getting quite fluent and so the conversation was free and effortless. They were both interested in the world outside Mato Grosso and plied me with questions about England and Hong Kong

I often wondered after the race how the stationmaster of a tiny station could afford to buy and maintain such a beautiful and obviously expensive horse. The answer came some time later when it was explained to me why it was that we always had to pay for the cattle trains in cash. In Brazil banks used to pay interest on all money held, even on checking accounts. The stationmasters would collect cash from the cattle companies, as well as from the normal passengers and keep the money in their own checking account until they had to submit their accounts and settle with the railway company. A lot of money changed hands as thousands of head of cattle were shipped along that railway line. I imagine that the interest accrued over the years padded their salaries nicely.

Fred.

19

A DEATH IN THE FAMILY, A RIDE THROUGH THE JUNGLE

As I mentioned earlier, the most poignant moment for me when I returned to Fazenda Estrela—Ligacao in my memory bank—was the memory of my dog Fred's death, there in the little house that had stood with little change all those years.

I had been on a fairly long ride out to the boundary, marked by a fairly substantial river. There had been some rain in the preceding week or two and the river was quite full. The two members of the commitiva who were with me persuaded me to stop for a swim where the river became a wide but fairly gentle rapids. We spent a little too long there enjoying the cool crystal clear water. Fred also loved it and was tearing around leaping over boulders and diving into the water, making great friends of the two cowboys, who at first were a little intimidated by his playfulness but soon joined him in his games. Because we had spent longer than we should we had to make the long journey back to the sede at a fairly fast walk instead of the slow relaxed amble that was customary. In my haste I failed to notice that Fred was lagging behind. After a while I turned to check on him and could not see him. I retraced my steps, to find him lying in the shade of a small tree, clearly exhausted. I rode the rest of the way with Fred draped across my saddle.

The next morning I realized that Fred was still not well so I left him at home to rest. In the evening I returned to find him clearly in distress, hardly able to recognize me. By nightfall Fred was labouring for breath although mercifully, at least for a while, sleeping. I kept a vigil by his bed with my hand resting lightly on his chest. This was partly for me to monitor his breathing but also to let him know that I was there; I felt that it was important that he knew that he was not alone. After a while he seemed to be easier and so, exhausted by the long vigil, I was able to fall asleep next to him. I was awakened later in the night, to find Fred walking around the room in a stupor, banging into things, seemingly oblivious of where he was; he had a frighteningly glazed look in his eyes and his mouth hung open, tongue hanging from one side. After some vain attempts to settle him down I could only watch in horror as he kept up his desperate walk. I knew my beloved dog was dying; the look of stark terror on his unseeing eyes, meant that he also knew it.

I took my .375 Mauser from the drawer by the bed and punched the magazine into place snapping the first bullet into the barrel. I sat in desperation on the cold stone floor of my Spartan bedroom. I stared at that wretched gun, knowing that I should help Fred out of his misery. The awful spectre of life without Fred rose before me. Mornings without that rousing bark, that I cursed each day, yet knew that I would miss; trailing cattle with my best cowboy, always just a shout away; but most of all, my best and really only friend. I must have raised that gun a dozen times yet could not shoot. A feeling of utter desperation came over me. I felt that I was being left behind by all that I held near and dear to me. I was very close, during that awful night, to using two bullets and ending two lives.

After a while Fred collapsed, so I carried him gently back to his bed. I lay with him, trying, as I had done previously when he had been poisoned in Tres Barros, to help him breath, this time I failed. Fred, my constant and loving companion was dead. I fell into an exhausted sleep, only to wake a short time later and face the full impact of what had happened.

The full realisation of my loss did not really hit me until later in the day. I asked one of the peons to dig a grave to bury Fred but first Peter agreed to do an autopsy. We needed to know why he had died; if it was a disease other animals could be at risk. Had it not been my dog, I would have done it but I could not bear the sight of my beloved dog, with his entrails hanging out. The result of the autopsy was severe heart damage; the whole heart was congested and blocked. He had obviously been suffering from a failing heart for some time. He was far too young for a heart attack and I was sure that the spraying episode on Tres Barros must have severely weakened his heart. I had ridden long distances with Fred by my side and that last ride had certainly not been the furthest; that part of the boundary was at a narrower part of the fazenda a long way short of the furthest boundaries.

On looking back I did recall one incident that should have made me take a closer look. Fred had a game he enjoyed which consisted of jumping to take a stick from my hand; the higher I held it the more he seemed to enjoy the game. A week or so before his death we had been playing but on the second jump he landed a little hard and let out a little grunt. Fred walked away, not wanting to play any more. His heart must have given him a little warning but I just thought that maybe he had landed wrong, slightly twisted something. When we were running around the rocks in the river he gave no signs of being anything other than a healthy happy dog. I was grateful that he did not suffer a long, drawn-out illness.

I went through the motions of working although my mind was not on anything except Fred. I returned to the house several times hoping that it had all been a nasty dream, and I would find him there wagging his tail in welcome.

Peter and Shirley Richardson invited me for dinner that night, knowing what I was going through. An evening with the Richardsons was usually a welcome change from my rather Spartan bachelor existence; Shirley was a great homemaker and I usually enjoyed the change. We all tried our hardest to make it a pleasant evening and I was very grateful to them for trying to cheer me up, but my pain was too great and my loss too real. Unfortunately Peter and Shirley left the next day for some leave, so I was desperately alone. It could not have happened at a worse time; I was made acutely aware of the complete isolation of a single 'Ingles' in the deepest interior of a foreign land. Although I was on friendly terms with many of the local people, being assistant manager, I had to remain slightly removed from them, even socially. The most innocent friendship could all too easily cause friction. The farm people would be quick to turn a harmless social visit into evidence of favour and little things can become mountains in such a small community. My evenings and weekends were spent in isolation. Ligacao was tolerable when I could visit the Richardsons, or take the dog out for a walk, or give him a bath, which was always an afternoon's entertainment. To suddenly find that I was alone in the middle of Mato Grosso, in a house that held bittersweet memories in every corner—be it scratch marks on the door, or the corner where he slept—became an awful strain. I found that I avoided the house as much as possible. The only thing to do was to find jobs that took me away from the sede. I rode with the commitiva whenever I could. I would stay the extra night in Rio Pardo when loading cattle. I could not stay away forever and always had to return to the house that was no longer a home. Fred's death was the turning point for me in Mato Grosso. I enjoyed the work and the place though I hated the loneliness, especially weekends, evenings and worst of all, the rainy days. We could have weeks of torrential rain. The ground would become so muddy and slippery that it was wise to stay at home or in the office, unless there was urgent business to force you to go outside.

Whenever I could find a reason to do so, I would visit one of the two other farms. I went to Lageada shortly after Fred's death, mainly to have a look at some virgin forest that had just been opened. I flew up this time, as I wanted to get an idea of the general topography from the air. We landed the plane at the airstrip and picked up the Brazilian manager and the foreman of the team that had cut the grid paths through the jungle. The flight to the area did not take long, and we flew around for a while, getting our bearings. The jungle trees were very tall and had ample foliage, so it was difficult sometimes to see the cuttings. There were areas where there had been some tree blight, which gave us some landmarks, as well as some idea of what the land looked like.

I stayed that night in the manager's house. It was a very pleasant bungalow, just a short walk away from the office. It was obviously quite an old house and rather picturesque, with a wide veranda all round. The house had a well-established tropical garden that seemed to reach into the house across the veranda.

Oswaldo Romero, the manager, was a man who had come up from cattle hand there in Lageada, to capitaz and then to the manager of the farm where he had been born. Oswaldo, in his late fifties and a little over weight, was still remarkably agile. He was clean-shaven but had a heavy shadow by the end of the day. His conversation did not stray far from affairs of the fazenda, of which he knew a great deal. His life, his entire world was there on Lageada and he knew little and cared less about the outside world. Oswaldo always wore a gun, a massive thing. The evenings I spent with him and his wife, a homely soul, who worshipped her man and catered to his every whim, were relaxed and casual affairs. We passed the evening on the wide veranda, enveloped by the aroma of the evening scent flowers as well as nature's night sounds that always seemed so close. Relaxed though we were, Oswaldo wore his gun. He would change into his pyjamas after dinner and return to the veranda for a last drink, with his gun belt in place over the pyjamas.

I was called early next morning and given a quick breakfast. We set out in the jeep to take a first hand look at the jungle we had flown over the day before. It was a long and tortuous drive, ending up at a very primitive retiro, headed by an old bugrie. The bugries were half Brazilian Indians. These people were as close as we got to employing the native Indians, who were occasionally to be seen in the jungle areas. The old man and his family had been born and raised right there where we found them. When the company started to develop the area, who better to use, than the people who knew the land intimately? We were greeted warmly by the old man and his wife and immediately supplied with a cup of almost treacle thick coffee. After a few minutes chatting, we mounted the horses that were waiting for us for the ride to the edge of the jungle, where we would meet the contractor who had opened the tracks. We headed the relatively short distance to the rendezvous, riding through some beautiful semi-jungle pastures. The trees were alive with macaws and parrots. Occasional clusters of virtually wild cattle could be seen hiding in the undergrowth. As a distant backdrop there stood the sheer granite face of the gigantic escarpments that bordered the fazenda. The jungle stood at the foot of the escarpment.

Our contractors had cleared a narrow strip of land, just wide enough to ride through, that crossed the jungle area in grid-like fashion. In this way we were able to get a good idea of the quality and lie of the land, as well as the types of trees that were there. The idea was to see whether it would be suitable for clearing for more pasture. If the trees were good, timber would help to pay for the clearing. I was not aware then of the importance of the rain forest and how I was being a part in its demise. When I returned to Mato Grosso recently, I was pleasantly surprised to learn that the Brazilian government had very strong regulations that required all farms to maintain a certain percentage of land as jungle. I saw thousand of acres on both the fazendas that were left for this purpose, including most of the jungle that I surveyed that day.

The sounds of the jungle are more fantastic than the sights. We were the intruders into a world that was not ours. Animal and birdcalls heralded our passage though we rarely saw a sign of life. Occasionally a bird would take to the air, and at one point a family of monkeys greeted us, or more likely taunted us, with screeches and howls accompanied be the shaking of branches. I was most impressed by the majesty of the tall hardwood trees that had stood their ground for, perhaps centuries. Their almost branchless trunks reached up into the canopy high above us, giving the effect of a vast cathedral. Oswaldo and the old bugrie were able to read signs from the jungle as we passed. They would show me where there were animal paths through the jungle, droppings or paw marks in the mud. We stopped at one point while the retireiro and the contractor led us off the path by foot to a place that was rich in herbs and plants, known for their medicinal use. Oswaldo collected a few of the plants to take home with him.

This was my first visit to the real jungle. I am not sure what I had expected, at least an encounter with a jaguar, or perhaps having to fight off an Anaconda. In reality jungle creatures are as afraid of us as we are of them, and wisely, prefer to keep their distance.

From time to time, as we rode through the cool twilight of the jungle, a break in the trees would give us a glimpse of the towering escarpment, like a huge mediaeval castle wall reaching high above us, reflecting the brilliant afternoon sun. It made a dramatic, brilliant orange backdrop to the darkened jungle below. Once we had finished our long, yet fascinating trip through the jungle, Oswaldo and I, having endured a further cup of treacly coffee, headed back towards the sede. On our way we stopped off at one of the retiros, where the commitiva had rounded up some of the herd that ran wild in the largely unfenced area.

The retiro itself was a very primitive affair, being little more than a staging point and corral for the outer most and wildest part of the farm. Every six months, an attempt was made to round up the herd that ran wild. This was done to sort out the male calves, castrate them, and bring them into the main herd of steers, which would eventually go down to the fattening farms in Sao Paulo. We also branded anything that was not branded. Sometimes, as on this occasion, mature and even old cows and bulls were found, that had never been branded, and had obviously never seen man before. A wild bull does not take kindly to being pushed around, especially when he is separated from the herd and enclosed in an unfamiliar environment like a corral. This was the scene that greeted us as we arrived at the corral. A large bull was cornered and snorting with rage and the cowboys were enjoying the challenge. A full rodeo was evolving. Our appearance put a slight dampener on the party but there was quite a lot of activity nonetheless. Mature cattle, finding themselves in an enclosed space, confronted by men with whips and loud voices can be very angry. Several times one of the commitiva would just make it over the corral wall before long and very lethal horns found their mark.

I returned to Ligacao by train, facing once more the reality of life without Fred. The lack of conversation, books and radio was never more significant than in those months following Fred's death. I tried to get interested in creating a little garden around my house, which helped to get my mind off the awful void that Fred had left.

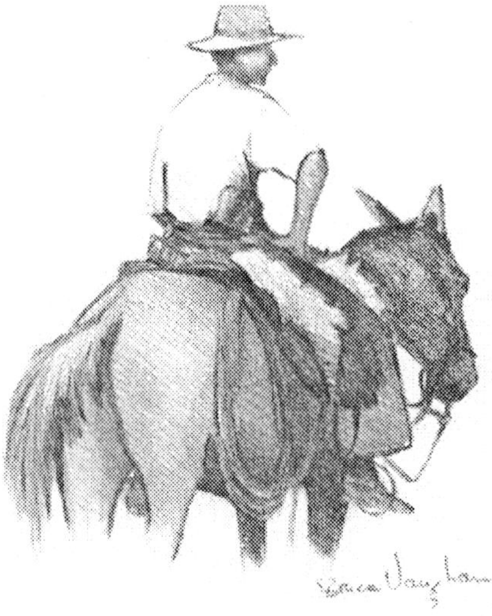

20

A WEDDING, NOT MINE AND AN ULCER, MINE

Managing a Brazilian fazenda did not stop at agriculture; in many ways it was like running a small country. Every house, building or road, man, woman, or child, came within the jurisdiction of the farm administration, As I gained more responsibility, I found myself having to oversee the building of a house, or corral, checking a new well, or making a map. The roads had to be kept as passable as possible; they were earth roads and were vulnerable to the weather; heavy rain would turn them into mud baths and the hot dry weather created long stretches of powdery sand. Wells had to be dug and maintained. I even found myself in the role of marriage councillor, dispute arbitrator or nurse to a sick child. If we had a dance on the farm, it was my job to attend and make sure that everyone checked in his or her guns and knives, before going in to the dance. I had to stay around to make sure that no fights started and no property damage was done. As a rule the dances were fairly quiet affairs though once in a while a few men would have a little too much to drink and fights would start, often over the most trivial argument. I did not try any heroics when this happened, instead ordered some of the less inebriated guests, to prise the fighters apart and usually we were able to send them on their way slightly bruised but otherwise intact.

One of the local farmers sent me an invitation to attend his daughter's wedding celebration. It was a big local event and everyone from a wide circumference was invited. I did not know the people very well, if at all. Napoleon, the office clerk, reminded me that the neighbour had sold us a couple of horses though I could not have picked him out of a line up. As they were neighbours, I felt that I must go and at least pay my respects, mainly so as to cause no ill feeling. A refusal could easily be interpreted as a slight. I did not want angry gun toting neighbours holding a grudge.

I arrived at the house, where the party had obviously been going for some time already and the mood was noisily festive. I was greeted by half the Ligacao cowboys, as well as by many cowboys and field hands from other farms, some of whom I recognized, many that I didn't. The farmer's house was a typical, very small and basic brick and plaster abode. Because of obvious limitation inside, the main party was happening outside between the house and the corral. There were tables stacked with food and bottles. A pit had been dug at one end of the clearing and a side of young beef was gradually losing its meat as it cooked slowly over the charcoal fire. I mingled with the crowd for a while, greeting my own people and being introduced to strangers. After a few minutes the father of the bride came over, threw his arms around me as if I was a long lost son. I of course pretended to recognize him although I could not for the life of me remember having seen him before, I had probably been more interested in the horses that he was trying to sell us, busy looking into their mouths. Dragging me by the arm, the father of the bride proudly invited me to come into the house to drink a toast to the young couple.

Amidst the scrupulously cleaned and scrubbed austerity of a typical Brazilian farmhouse, the now familiar scene met my eyes. Two children sat shyly on two stiff-backed chairs that had been draped with the best tablecloth for the occasion. They were dressed as if they had just returned from their high-school graduation exercises. They were probably between fourteen and fifteen, the girl, as usual, was younger than the boy. I had seen this before yet I still felt awkward about it. At least these kids seemed to be a little older than some of the couples I had seen in the past. I sat near them; feeling as embarrassed as they were looking, while the mothers of the two pressed me with neat brandy and rather sickly snacks. They hovered over me and kept filling my glass again the moment I took the smallest sip. Having exhausted my powers of conversation and conviviality whilst smiling until my face hurt, I found some way to excuse myself and made for the door.

I could hear even before I left the house that the party was getting a little noisy. There seemed to be a good deal of heated conversation, which was not in keeping with the festive nature of the gathering. Even had I been stone cold sober I would have still been totally unprepared for what was about to happen. I had decided to make straight for the jeep, which was parked under a tree across from the sede. I had done my duty to both families and met the newly weds, and had quite a long way to drive back to Ligacao. When I came out of the house I aimed my, already slightly muzzy head and hopefully body, towards my vehicle, concentrating seriously on my gait as well as my direction.

It dawned on me after a while that there was nobody between the jeep and myself. It was as if the crowd had parted to give me room. I also became aware that there was a whole lot of shouting coming from either side of me, angry shouting, out of place on such a festive occasion. At this point the first gun went off, followed by a barrage of shots from both sides. I sobered instantly and beat the record for the hundred-yard dash to the jeep. I started the engine and drove out in a cloud of dust.

I inquired the following day from the men, whether anyone had been hurt but they assured me that most of the shots had been fired into the air in intimidation or just excitement and that nobody had been hit. They also seemed unable to remember what the argument had been about.

It was a very unhealthy habit in up-country Brazil for cowboys to express their pleasure, displeasure or general excitement by firing their guns into the air. The horse race incident was just one occasion when I had been too close when cowboys had, through anger or excitement fired their guns into the air. I always wondered where those bullets came down, imagining cattle or even people being struck by a vertically directed bullet.

In spite of, or perhaps because of, my desperate attempts to stay occupied, my health started to take a definite down turn. On the face of things, I had everything that a person could want. My house was spacious, although not luxurious though more than adequate. I had a large garden, which was beginning to look respectable, although it still mainly consisted of a large well-kept lawn. If I had wanted a bigger garden, I could have just asked someone to move the fence. I was, in Peter's absence, master of all I surveyed. My personal horses were ready whenever I needed them and I had a jeep sitting in the garage. In most parts of the world, to have all this would be the mark of a very wealthy man. There was, however a desperate loneliness and an urge for company. The nearest town was Campo Grande; three hours drive, on a good day. In the dry season the sand of the road was so powdery that it could be very treacherous. If you stopped in the very dry sand you could just stay there. If you tried to drive out the wheels just dug a deeper hole. The only way to drive through powdery sand is to keep a constant speed. When it came to corners, you just had to bounce off the side of the ruts and never, never stop or even slow down. In the wet season the road became pure mud and previous small streams could become raging rivers that flooded the road. One extreme season seemed to run into another.

Fred's death, coupled with the long absence of the only people I could socialize with, was a definite factor in my depression. Each morning I found myself almost incapable of dragging myself out of bed. I had to be at the office, which was about one hundred yards from my house, at five-thirty in the morning. The men were assembled at that time and after conferring with the capitaz, orders were given and jobs allotted. Each morning as I started out for the office, I was able to make it to the front door but when the cold morning air hit me, I was hit by a wave of nausea and started to gag. I braced myself for the walk, relying on trees and fence posts to steady me and often nearly collapsed. It was a major struggle each morning to close those one hundred yards from my house to the office.

The Richardsons finally returned and immediately realized that something was drastically wrong. I was packed off to Campo Grande to see the local doctor. Having listed my various symptoms to the good doctor, who faithfully wrote them all down; I was given one set of pills for each symptom and sent home. "Oh! The wonders of medical science".

The medicine had turned me into a zombie and Peter decided that I should go down to Sao Paulo for a complete check-up. He was in the process of dictating a letter to his wife, who acted as his secretary, while I was sitting at my desk desperately trying to concentrate on doing some figures in the stock book. The page started to swim in front of my eyes and then slowly and quietly the desk as well as the room seemed to rotate ninety degrees. Then there was darkness. I came round on the office floor, with several worried faces peering down at me. I was packed onto the daily flight to Sao Paulo the following evening.

After exhaustive tests it was decided that I had an ulcer. After a week or so in hospital, I was set free with a strict diet to follow. Head office decided to send me down to their banana estate. This was decided firstly, because they had a very pleasant rest house there, where I could rest up and be looked after for a while. Secondly, because they had some peripheral land, unsuitable for bananas and they were interested in starting a small breeding herd there. I was told that when I felt well enough to get back to work, I could start forming a little Tres Barros down in Fazenda Sao Sebastian. It was a beautiful little coastal farm, named after the island of Sao Sebastiao. It was in fact on the mainland, situated almost half way between Santos and Rio de Janeiro. After a two-day visit to Ligacao to pack up my belongings, I returned to Sao Paulo and then travelled down by an express bus to the nearest town to Sao Sebastiao called Carraguatatuba. I was grateful for a short break in the town, after a hair-raising ride down the winding mountain road from the Sao Paulo plateaux. We stopped in Carraguatatuba just long enough for me to see that it was a very small though quite charming little seaside town. Before we left Carraguatatuba, I asked the bus driver to let me know where I should get off for the 'fazenda dos Ingles" as the locals referred to it. The bus continued down the coast road that would pass the entrance to the farm. About fifteen minutes out of town, the driver called over his shoulders that we were coming to my stop.

It was already evening when we pulled up at a junction that seemed to be deserted. There was no light or sign of life, as far as I could see. I thanked the driver as I set my cases, beloved saddle and recently acquired lasso by the side of the road. The bus, my only link with the world, rattled off down the road and was soon out of sight. Except for the distant surf pounding on a beach nearby, there wasn't a sight or a sound to break the stillness of the night. I waited for what seemed like an age looking hopefully in all directions in search of life. I was just about making up my mind to try walking but still had not decided in which direction, when I saw headlights coming through some trees along the junction road. It was the company driver, who greeted me and took me to the guesthouse, some twenty minutes away by road. There a delightful, jolly, buxom lady, along with her large family of smiling and giggling children, welcomed me and showed me to my room. The children fought over who was to carry my bags, even my wide-brimmed hat was taken from me and worn proudly by the smallest boy. After a quick shower and change from my travelling clothes, the good lady placed a welcome meal before me. The entire family gathered around the table, although they had obviously eaten earlier, and I ate as dozens of eyes watched me. Between mouthfuls, I had to answer the most detailed and searching questions about my life. I enjoyed the company however as well as the novelty of being in a home full of people, instead of rattling around in an empty house. I had been limited to my own company for far too long and found the novelty of company a bit overwhelming. After a while I wished them all good night and went off to bed. In spite of the journey and the welcome committee I felt relaxed and happy to just let things happen.

The office and rail cars. Sao Sebastiao.

21

THE IMPORTANCE OF THE FIRST IMPRESSION

I was wearing my full-length boots, baggy Gaucho trousers and wide brimmed hat, somewhat out of place on a banana plantation; however I did not want people to mistake me for a fruit man. I stood watching the narrow gauge railway tracks for the small, white-canopied rail car that would contain my new manager. The rails danced in the heat, as they cut a track straight through the lush green banana groves for at least a mile, before blending in with the foliage. Beyond the bananas stood the granite knoll where the English staff had their houses, perched high above the farm with an uninterrupted three hundred and fifty degree view from mountain peaks to the Atlantic Ocean. From my standpoint I would be able to see the little rail car well in advance and so be prepared to make a good first impression. The track was empty but, as will always happens at the most inopportune moment, my bladder was full. I did not want to meet the company's senior fruit manager with my legs crossed and my eyes bulging, so I asked where it was and headed for the little outhouse behind the office buildings.

With nature appeased and my confidence restored, I prepared to return to my vigil. I slid the bolt and tried the door, it did not move; the door was firmly jammed. This cannot be happening, I thought. It is just a bad dream. Perhaps there really was some curse—probably a hangover from a previous life—as it was the third time I had been locked in a toilet.

THE IMPORTANCE OF THE FIRST IMPRESSION

I took a deep breath, so as not to panic; then I panicked. I pounded on the door and then stood on the toilet seat and shouted through the little window near the ceiling. The nearest building housed the huge electric generators, which gave power to the packing plants, offices and residents. It also gave off a steady, noisy hum. My cries for help went unheard.

I calmed myself and took stock of my situation. There was one jammed door and a small window covered with mosquito netting between my now desperate self and freedom. Clearly the line of least resistance lay through the window, small and high thought it was. I soon had the edge of the wire netting freed enough to squeeze through. Using the toilet seat as a launching pad, I started to climb headfirst through the window.

What goes up of course must come down. Going up headfirst is one thing however coming down headfirst is a different matter altogether. As I emerged through the window, I found that the ground was a lot further from the window than the top of the toilet seat had been, and it looked very hard and unyielding. I was at the point-of-no-return, hanging from the waist, with no way of pushing myself backwards. To complicate matters my belt had become hooked onto one of the nails that secured the frame of the mosquito net. I couldn't go back, and even if I had wanted to, I couldn't go forward.

Mr. Vernon Braham and I met almost exactly on schedule, only the venue had changed. I was eyeball to eyeball with the man I most wanted to impress but he had me at a distinct disadvantage. My eyeballs were upside down at the time and bulging considerably.

"You must be young Vaughan."

I smiled and assured him that I was indeed he. "I am sorry I was not at the office when you arrived, Sir but I was held up." I tried a little levity to break the tension; the only thing that broke was the nail that held me, and I fell in a crumpled heap at the manager's feet.

"I don't know why you can't use the door like normal people," he said. I did not like the way he emphasized 'normal'.

"It was the door, Sir," I stuttered, as I rose trying desperately to adjust my dress and regain my composure. "It jammed". I gave it a push to illustrate my point and it swung open effortlessly.

My new boss was probably close to sixty, diminutive, bald, bronzed by the Brazilian sun and heavily wrinkled yet still possessed great energy and mental agility.

In spite of the rather poor start, we spent a busy day together viewing the areas of grassland that fringed the banana estate. The land that had been earmarked for future dairy farm was scattered around the edges of the banana groves and extended well up into the foothills that made up three of the boundaries to the property, the fourth was the South Atlantic Ocean. My assignment, once I felt up to it, was to turn these grasslands, which were of no use for bananas or sugar cane, into a small milk producing dairy farm.

I had the distinct feeling that Mr. Braham had been opposed to the idea although he had accepted head office's decision and was giving it his best. This was my first solo assignment and I was eager to make a go of it.

It was a beautiful estate, nestling in a deep valley with quite high mountains reaching up on either side. The flat base of the valley was chequered with the lush green of the banana fields. The slightly less steep foothills that bordered the estate had been cleared some time ago and long grass grew on the slopes. These slopes and a few areas of flat land were to be my cattle farm. Pastures were often tucked away in little unused corners of the estate, so I could see that things were going to be a little difficult. As we parted, Mr. Braham invited me to dinner, promising to send the jeep to collect me later.

The manager's house stood on the high knoll that I had seen that morning. The house and surrounding garden commanded a spectacular view of the entire estate that spread out from the foot of the knoll. Immediately beyond the estate an impressive range of mountain peaks created a dramatic backdrop. I was able to see some of the slopes that we had ridden up that morning. The sea view was equally exciting. We looked out at the endless expanse of azure sea, still well lit by the early evening light. Once the view had been duly admired, Mr. Braham, no sign that I should call him Vernon, armed me with a drink and led me to the sitting room that opened up onto a veranda. We could hear the distant Atlantic breakers crashing themselves onto the sands many feet below us as we struggled to keep a conversation going. It was hard work; we found that the legendary, pioneer, fruit manager had little to say to an upstart cattleman. And the reverse was equally true.

The pauses were getting longer, as we both struggled for something to talk about. I was getting more and more uncomfortable, as the sofa I was sitting on just did not seem to suit any sitting position. My host must have noticed my discomfort.

"That is a new sofa," he remarked. "But it doesn't seem to be quite right somehow."

"Let me take a look," I said, desperate for a way of avoiding further conversation. After a quick examination I had the fault diagnosed. Demonstrating great leadership potential and self-confidence, I called for a screwdriver, and started to dismantle the sofa. The venerable fruit manager was soon on his knees beside me, caught up in the enthusiasm. Together we quickly had the sofa in bits, scattered over the Persian rug. My diagnosis, as it turned out, had been wrong; it was in fact just a very uncomfortable sofa.

"We'll soon have it back together again," I said, reassuringly, and we set to to rectify the situation. Dinner was delayed a little, to allow us time to solve the jigsaw, and then delayed some more as patience ran into impatience and then exasperation.

Dinner started badly. We seemed no nearer to putting that sofa back together after the delays, than we had been before. There was a definite cooling in our relationship, not that it had been exactly warm before.

Conversation, which had never been our strong point, was reduced to the barest essentials, and even then somewhat curt. Making tiredness or a headache an excuse, my host decided to retire early, handing me the keys of his jeep. He suggested that I drive myself back to the guesthouse without further delay.

"Thank you very much for the dinner, Sir," I said brightly. "Perhaps I should come again some evening, when we have more time, and help you get that sofa fixed."

I was sitting behind the wheel of the jeep, before Mr. Braham found words although I am not sure what they were, as he was mumbling unintelligibly. There was a heavy rainstorm as I drove back, which makes driving on earth roads very tricky. I found myself sliding from one side of the road to another, with the jeep making the decisions. I was not familiar with the road at the best of times and this was not one of them. I could see that the road dipped, before turning fairly sharply to the left. I tried to slow down but it made no difference. I turned the wheel, which merely caused the jeep to approach the corner sideways. Both right-hand wheels sank deep into the far ditch and there they remained, in spite of four-wheel drive and reduced gear. I walked the last mile to my lodgings.

"Hello, is that Mr. Braham?" I asked when a sleepy voice answered the telephone.

"Yes it is; who is that?" The voice was far from friendly.

"This is Bruce Vaughan, Sir," I tried to keep a smile in my voice but it got no further than the teeth.

"Well"

"I just wanted to thank you again for the evening", I blurted, "and to assure you that I got through that rainstorm alright. I thought you might have worried." I added naively.

"Ah ha!"

"Oh yes, about the jeep. It is alright but seems to be a little bit stuck at the corner at the bottom of the hill." I took a quick breath and then plunged on, "I shall go back in the morning to get it out."

"Don't go anywhere near that jeep." The telephone seemed to jump in my hand. "I'll send the driver." There was a click and the phone was dead.

22

A LITTLE TRES BARROS

I took Mr. Braham's advice and lay very low for the next couple of weeks on health grounds. The beach was beautiful and usually quite deserted. It was about a ten-minute walk from the end of the little railway line that was the lifeline for the estate. Each of the section managers had their own little rail car and there were some that took workers or stores along the line. Larger trains were used for transporting the bananas from the fields to packing station and from there to the jetty for shipping. I was usually able to thumb a ride and then walk out to the beach for a day of just doing nothing in the shade of a tree, or frolicking in the waves, which were quite good for body surfing. I was able to borrow some books from the British staff and catch up on some reading. I loved the feeling of being on holiday; I was in reality on sick leave. It was the first break I had had since joining the company and I was determined to enjoy it. I was invited to dinner by some of the other expats and started to feel as if I belonged. After a while I began to tire of my freedom, inaction and lack of direction; I hankered to get on with the job.

The months that followed were the most interesting and challenging, and thereby enjoyable of my Brazilian tour. Once I had regained my health, I plunged myself into the task of creating a breeding herd in Sao Sebastiao. The land that was allocated to me was mainly the hilly area around the boundary of the bananas that I had toured on my first day, as well as some areas on the flat that were not suitable for bananas, although they were still liable to flooding. There was just a nucleus of a herd already, mainly there for milk and butter for the estate personnel. There was also an area set aside for horses and mules, which were to come under my command. The local people were mainly untrained in cattle and not too many had even ridden a horse before; so I really had to start from scratch.

My first job was to find myself a capitaz and then get him to round up a few more, experienced cattlemen, so that we could at least get started. In time these first few could help to train some of the locals. A capitaz miraculously fell into my hands within a few days.

A lean, weathered and rather sinister looking man in his fifties, wearing a battered hat, threadbare shirt, trousers and boots that were falling apart, was squatting against the farm office wall when I arrived at the main office one morning. One of the clerks told me that a peon was looking for me; he indicated, almost reluctantly and definitely disapprovingly, the squatting figure that I had noticed outside.

Joao Pereira had heard that I was looking for a man with experience and he had come running. Joao had had his own small farm in Goias but had got himself badly in debt and had had to sell. He was bought out by a big organisation, probably for a song, barely giving him enough to clear his debts. Joao had been kept on as a capitaz for a few years and then the land had been requisitioned by the Government to build the President's dream capital, Brasilia. I am sure that the new owners were well compensated, and it may have been the reason they had bought it from Joao, who would have had no idea of its potential worth. So he was without a job. After trying to establish a small business in Caraguatatuba, our nearby town, where he had relatives, Joao had gone bankrupt for the second time and was working as a casual labourer. At first I took Joao's hard luck story with a pinch of salt. I agreed to take him on, on a temporary basis, however after a few days I knew that I had found my man.

Joao wrote to a friend of his in Goias, asking him to come down to join him, suggesting that he bring a few saddles and lassoes etc with him. Without bothering to reply, Pedro arrived from Goias, with a box full of Brazilian saddles and trappings of varying ages though all quite usable. I bought some of them for the farm, and he sold the others to our budding cattlemen. Pedro was a cheerful, tall, gangling man in his late forties. Joao and Pedro soon became a great team and we were able to start forming our farm in earnest.

Some of the hilly slopes had been planted in grass at various stages, partly to stop erosion after slopes had been cleared of jungle, and partly in preparation for the forming of a herd. We therefore had the pastureland, now we had to work out the details of getting cattle from one place to another. The banana areas were honeycombed with irrigation ditches, and interspersed with swampy areas. The only means of access to many areas was by the miniature railway. I could not see Mr. Braham allowing us to herd cattle along the line, or to use his banana carriages as cattle wagons. We had to cut cattle trails along the foothills, sometimes going all the way round a valley that you could almost throw a stone across.

Our first objective was to get one retiro functioning and then start opening others, as and when we had the men and the cattle to do so. Using our small domestic herd as our first retiro, we examined each cow, calf and bull; selling anything that did not meet our standard, which was of necessity not too high at this juncture. We scouted around the Caraguatatuba and Ubatuba area and were able to buy one or two head from smallholdings but not enough to replace the cattle we had sold. We gathered together a small group of men, mostly inexperienced, however they were all keen to help Joao, Pedro and I, in what was becoming a focal point of local interest. We had no shortage of applicants from dozens of would-be John Waynes, so we were able to pick and choose.

Once we had finished culling out the cattle, we found that it was becoming a cattle farm without cattle, or horses. The few horses we had were of poor quality and untrained in cattle work. I sent a report to Sao Paulo and requested the funds to go up into the plateau country where the best dairy herds were to be found. I received a reasonable budget and set out with Joao, leaving Pedro in command, and headed for the hills.

The temperature on the plateau was noticeably cooler than at sea level, with lush pastures and fat contented cattle. It was raining lightly and slightly misty, reminding me of the farm country around Tiverton in Devon, where I had spent most of my youth. We visited numerous small farms, within a fairly wide area. At night we stayed in small pensions or inns, starting out each morning at dawn so as to be able to catch the milking and see the cows and calves together. We were usually welcomed with open arms, mainly because our credit was good, being backed by one of the biggest cattle companies in Brazil. Prices always started high, and after hours of bartering, feigning horror, threatening to leave—like buying food in a Chinese market—we eventually came down to a workable price. At this point the farmer was either prepared to sell, or admitted that he would only have been prepared to sell, had we paid his exorbitant price. Whatever the outcome we all shook hands and separated as friends, complimenting each other on our knowledge of cattle and prices.

Joao was a great help. He knew his cattle and his horses, and proved incorruptible. He told me at two of the farms, that the owner had offered him a percentage if he were to get me to agree to a higher price. On both occasions we left without buying. After five days of farm hopping, we had accumulated six horses and about thirty cows, some with calf and most already serviced and in varying stages of pregnancy.

We had spent the last day of our trip at a fairly large farm and after much good humoured bartering, had bought several cows and a couple of very good horses. Having concluded our business, we were invited to have lunch at the owner's house. Before going in to lunch we were strolling around the sede with the owner, when I noticed that there was a large fenced off area, with an Alsatian bitch and four very young pups.

Seeing my interest in the puppies, the farmer asked, "Would you like to take a look at them?"

"Yes, Senhor. I used to have an Alsatian but he died a few months ago. I miss him greatly." I replied.

"Let's go." He led me over to the gate. The bitch ran towards us and jumped up barking madly but I noticed that in spite of all the bravado, her tail was wagging. I opened the gate, went into the run and started picking up the pups and playing with them. The bitch came over licked the pup I was holding and then licked me. I came out from the run, congratulating the owner on such fine pups, to find that the owner and Joao had been scared out of their wits when I had entered the run. They both thought that the bitch would go for me. During lunch we discussed Alsatians, as well as cattle and farming in general. As we were leaving, the farmer disappeared for a moment, and then returned with a basket, which he put into the back of my jeep. I really had not given any thought of replacing Fred, so it was something of a shock for me when the food hamper, in the back of the jeep started to yap, just as we were driving away from the farm. I had, it seemed, acquired another Alsatian pup. This time it was a female, about two months old and as cute as all get out. So it was that Lindy came into my life.

We had arranged for a local cattle trucker to collect and transport the cattle and horses, from the various farms. We set a date a few days away, to give us time to get ready to receive them. We were then free to return to Sao Sebastiao, tired yet excited and very satisfied with the result of our buying trip. With our new cattle arriving within a few days, we had a number of last minute details to clear up. All the cattle were going to a new retiro, so we had to be prepared for everything, from milking stools upwards. Pedro agreed to become temporary retireiro, with a younger trainee under him. We hoped to replace Pedro within a few months, either by his trainee or hopefully someone with more experience, if we could find one. We needed Pedro to help us with the rest of the farm.

We had chosen to put our second retiro where it was, because it had access by road from the outside. In this way the lorry could come in direct. It had been agreed that the trucks would collect the various batches of cattle and horses, and bring them to one central point one evening and then reload them all early the following morning. In this way they would travel in the coolest part of the day. On the day of their arrival, Joao and I went down early to the retiro. We had to rush around and do all the little things that had been forgotten, or left to the last moment. One of our over sights was the water supply, which needed a small pump, to pump water from the well. We had one on order but it had not yet arrived. We rigged up a temporary hand-pump for immediate use. Our prize herd finally arrived in three trucks. They were a rather mixed assortment of cows and calves as well as the horses. They were a far cry from the thousands of almost identical Zebu steers that I had been used to receiving in Mato Grosso. These, however, were very special cattle. They were hand picked and were the pride of the farm, at least in my eyes.

Retiro Two, with Pedro in command was now in business. My main worry was whether the animals would suffer from the heat, as the temperature at sea level was quite a bit higher than on the plateau where they had just come from. They seemed to make out quite well. Mr. Braham paid us a surprise visit to look at the new cattle and see how the retiro was functioning. He was obviously quite pleased and I felt that I had regained at least some respect. I had the feeling that I was still under close scrutiny. I had not been invited back for dinner.

One of my favourite rides was up the steepest of the hill-pastures, through the eucalyptus trees at the foot of the hill and then along a path that gradually climbed up into the upper slopes. It was a beautiful ride; from there I could look over the entire farm with its many shades of green and then beyond to the turquoise and blue of the sea beyond. I felt like King Henry Christophe surveying his Haitian kingdom. I spent many hours riding up in the hill slopes, mapping the pastures, seeking new areas for the future and often planning future retiro sites, from as near to an aerial view as I could hope for. The farm occupied an entire valley, bordered on the landside by the high peaks that reached thousands of feet, continuing up to the higher levels of the Sao Paulo plateau. The remaining border was the road that I had come along in the bus. Beyond which a few hundred yards of scrubland separated the farm from the beach. I was able to see the coast from my vantage point, plus many miles of Atlantic rollers, spanning the horizon, ending their long journey as white foam on the Brazilian coastline.

All the pastures were badly in need of weeding but owing to the nature of the land, this had to be done by hand. Progress was very slow, partly due to an acute lack of labour-force. I had to borrow some weeders from the Banana section but the greatest factor was the cost. My budget was far from generous. Seeing the weeds growing faster than we could get to them made me very impatient. Many were the times that I left my horse under a tree and, wielding my long knife, worked off my frustrations on the scrub weeds. One day when a local farmer came looking for me to sell us some cattle, he found me stripped to the waist slashing at some high weed bushes. He watched in unmasked amazement, while I continued slashing, unaware of his presence. Joao, who had brought him to meet me, finally called me and we returned to the sede to look at the cows that he had brought, entirely on spec, in the hopes that I would buy them. They were quite presentable, so we went to the office to discuss cattle prices. I used the situation to cut through a lot of bartering, by pointing out that we were under such a tight budget, that even the manager had to do the weeding, so we came down to a reasonable price very quickly.

As retiro two settled down we were able to expand further and several buying trips followed. I sent Joao alone on one extensive trip to get enough cattle for at least one retiro if not two. He returned a week later obviously very pleased with himself, with sixty head of cattle for far less than we had budgeted for. There were two more horses included to boost our stable. I was pleased with our progress and sent a report up to Roddy Taylor in Sao Paulo to let him know what was happening.

Pegasus.

23

PEGASUS

We were able to acquire some more horses from neighbouring farms as well as those that came from the plateau. Our number of cowboys was increasing and the need for horses was mounting. I spent most of my day on horseback, so I needed three horses. My favourite mount was in fact not one of the ones we had bought from the plateau but a creamy white stallion that Mr. Braham had bought from a local farmer some time previously, who used him to pull a cart. The poor stallion had been in a very poor condition, as he had been worked almost to death when Mr. Braham noticed him. In his youth Mr. Braham had been a very keen horseman and he knew his horses. When he first saw this poor creature he was clearly in a shocking condition, but Mr. Braham had the feeling that given proper treatment, the stallion still possessed great potential. After the usual bleeding and a couple of months out to pasture the stallion started to blossom again. His body filled out and his coat started to regain its previous shine.

Mr. Braham decided he was ready to ride. After saddling the stallion, he was ready to mount but as soon as he put his foot in the stirrup, the stallion reared up sending the ageing, rather diminutive Mr. Braham sprawling onto the corral floor. He valiantly tried several times to get into the saddle, with the same humiliating result. This happened whenever anyone tried to ride him, and there were several takers; so after a few rather bruised bodies and fractured egos, the stallion was left out in the pasture growing fat, lazy and content—probably not content, more frustrated, as I am sure that he wanted to do more than just vegetate.

Once I set eyes on the stallion I also knew that he was by far the best animal on the farm. He must have had a name at some time though nobody knew what it was, so I decided to call him Pegasus because he seemed to prefer flying. I brought Pegasus into the corral and after a little trouble, was able to get him quietened down enough to saddle him. I allowed him a few moments to get used to wearing a saddle once more; then came the moment of truth. I had listened carefully to all the tales of his rearing as soon as anyone put their foot into the stirrup, and decided that what was needed was a little subterfuge and cunning. After talking gently to my quarry and passing my hand along his neck, I tried a light pressure on the seat of the saddle, there was very little reaction but as soon as I put a little downward pressure on the stirrup Pegasus started to rear. I quickly calmed him again then, whilst petting him with one hand, I gathered the reins in the other hand plus a little mane and then I jumped into the saddle without touching the stirrups. The stallion was taken by surprise but started to buck and rear a moment later. He was too late; I was in the saddle and now in command.

After only a few moments of rearing and snorting and tossing his head, Pegasus started to gallop around the corral. I was afraid that he might try to get me off by brushing past the planking so I held his head into the corral side to make sure that he could not see the fence that well. After some firm pressure on the reins and some reassuring words, Pegasus came under control. We fell in love. Well I fell in love. We had to go through this little jumping device every time I got on but once I was in the saddle he was a dream. I am sure that Pegasus must have come from the cattle farms on the plateau, as he could work cattle instinctively; he was as good as any cattle horse I had known up country. He obviously had not been working cattle for some time and was delighted to once more be doing something he was used to.

From time to time I had to go to the main office, where I was never without an audience once I had finished my business and was preparing to remount Pegasus. Probably many a bet was laid on the outcome of each mount. The first time I rode to the sede with him, we arrived with a bit of gusto. Just as we were crossing the railway line, Pegasus was spooked by the sound of an oncoming rail cab. He jumped high into the air, and we did a couple of turns round the factory yard, before he came under control again. I tethered him outside the office while I did what I had come for and then got ready to leave. A few curious office staff followed me out, as the stallion's reputation was already quite well known on the estate. When I remounted we went through our customary drama and then departed as we had arrived, leaving a trail of dust.

Perhaps my most embarrassing moment whilst astride Pegasus, was when he decided to make an amorous pass at one of the mares and I found myself, for a few precarious moments trying to maintain my dignity along with my balance, until he had had his way with the mare

I had several horses in my string, as I was riding most of each working day although Pegasus was always my great favourite. Pegasus was quite a bit taller than most of the other horses and a lot taller than some, so I rode head and shoulders above the other cowboys, giving me great status.

I only came to grief once with Pegasus. We were crossing one of the many railway bridges, which only had planking between the lines for us to walk on. In hindsight I should have got off and led him across but as we had to cross these quite often, and regularly did so without incident, I felt safe. As we were about half way across, Pegasus stepped on a loose plank, panicked and jumped sideways. We ended up both on our backs in the swamp below the bridge. It took a lot of coaxing to get Pegasus back to dry land. I tried to avoid bridges with him for a time after that, as he was, understandably, quite nervous for a while. He settled down again quite quickly and became quite used to the tracks and the rail traffic. He even watched disinterestedly as rail cars or even banana trains passed us just a few feet away, as we rode along the narrow paths next to the rail. Going along the railway lines saved us a lot of time getting from one part of the estate to the other, the alternative was to go all the way round.

24

THE HOUSE ON THE HILL AND THE JEEP WITH NO SEAT

After my first few weeks on the farm, during which I stayed at the guesthouse, a house was made ready for me. I bade my farewell to the delightful family at the guesthouse that had looked after me so well. They had done everything possible to make my stay pleasant. The children seemed genuinely sad to see me go; I had been a source of great interest and I suppose entertainment. I had enjoyed their company as well, especially after the loneliness of Ligacao. I moved into a large wooden house, not far from the rest house, perched on the very top of a fairly high knoll, overlooking the main office and surrounded by a sea of banana groves. The remainder of the English management staff lived on the larger knoll quite a distance from the office.

My house had a view almost as spectacular as some of my favourite hill slope vantage points that I enjoyed whilst out riding. I was not able to see the sea from my house but I had a three-hundred-and-sixty-degree view of the farm and mountains. It was a bit incongruous to have the cattle division manager situated in the midst of the bananas, however this was the best that was available at the time and cattle were fairly low on the priorities list at San Sebastiao. A long column of steps led up from the road level near the office and factory, which, although I never counted them—definitely in the hundreds, I felt like a Hindu pilgrim visiting the Batu Caves temple in Malaysia—they seemed to be never ending; rendering me exhausted even before reaching the top. Having climbed these steps once, I quickly made arrangements for one of my horses to be brought up each morning to the house. A young would-be cowboy rode up with my horse in tow, using the longer route via a winding pathway that curled around the knoll. I could now start my day by riding down in a more leisurely and definitely more dignified fashion and end it by riding up again, which made my mountain perch far more acceptable.

The house that was allotted to me was a good-sized, wooden bungalow with three bedrooms and one wide veranda that went all the way round. It was built to follow the contour of the hill, so that some rooms were on different levels. Lindy and I, once she had moved in and taken over, had plenty of room to move about in, including a reasonable area of garden. The garden had been well planned by who ever had lived there before, although it was then a bit overgrown and run down. With a cook and housemaid to look after us, our worldly needs were well catered for. The main problem was that we were a long way from any other 'expat' houses, and no one ever popped up the hundreds of steps to pay me a surprise visit. Once I had climbed or ridden up the hill for the night, socially I might just as well have been in the Sahara desert. There was no telephone, radio or of course television. I had a Grundig tape recorder and a few tapes that I had brought from England which were the extent of my home entertainment.

Recreational transport was another problem, as I only had use of one of the little rail cars on a share basis, with the most junior of the English banana section people, and then only during working hours. My co-user needed it to return to the other end of the farm each evening. There were two jeeps on the estate. One was the manager's and the other was the jeep that I had used for the buying trips. The remainder of the English banana people shared this second jeep, with rank having the most pull. Once in a while I made the long trip by horse into Caraguatatuba to do a little essential shopping, and once somewhat illegally by jeep.

The shared jeep was parked at the factory for a few days, while it was being fixed and then repainted. The seats had been taken out and were being recovered; the jeep was sitting there over the weekend waiting to be painted on Monday. I placed a fruit box where the driver's seat should be and headed out for a secret, illicit night on the town. I had a great time driving around the town while there was still light, enjoying the ambience of a small and rather quiet seaside resort town. I then spent the evening exploring the local high spots, or at least the highest spots that Caraguatatuba had to offer—not very high by anyone's standard. All went well until, on the return journey, I came round a corner a little faster than I should have and the fruit box slid away from me. Suddenly all I could see was the night sky and some trees. I struggled to regain control of the car though not before losing a bit of paint on a fence post. I made sure that I parked the jeep in the exact spot I had found it and then removed the grass and leaves stuck to the mudguard. It was going to be repainted so the minor scratches would soon disappear. I was really in no fit state to climb back to my mountain retreat but I made it somehow.

By and large the fact that I was relatively isolated did not worry me much, I started early in the morning and often worked until late in the evening. On Sunday mornings I would sleep in as late as I could but, as I was used to being out and about by five or six in the morning, I always found that sleep after this time was difficult even if I knew it was Sunday. Lindy thankfully was not such a taskmaster as Fred had been and she took her cue from me, if I lay in she was happy to do so too. Invariably by midmorning I was restless. I sometimes ended up going down to the nearest retiro and finding some excuse to do something. There was usually a sick calf to tend to, or perhaps some more weeds to dig. After lunch I relaxed and read, or did some drawing. In the cool of the early evening, I would sometimes go down to the field near the factory, to play football or perhaps swim in the river that passed at the foot of my knoll. Sometimes the thought of the climb back caused me to reconsider.

There was some socialising amongst the fruit 'expats', however I was situated at the opposite end of the farm to the rest of them. It usually required a definite invitation and the arrangement of transport. I found that the best way to be invited was to invite one of them to come to my house for dinner. The prospect of having to climb the hundreds of steps up to my knoll was enough to produce an alternative venue. I only knew one of the English 'expats' prior to my arrival. David Harrison had been on Tres Barros for a short while before being posted to Sao Sebastiao. Although I had met him at the little clubhouse I did not really know him very well. David was the number two, in charge of the replanting and new areas of bananas being opened up. I remembered his excitement prior to leaving Tres Barros when he thought that he was to take over as manager of Sao Sebastiao. I heard from the others that he had been very disappointed and a little bitter at first, but finally resigned himself to the fact that although he was the heir apparent, like royalty, he had to wait for death or retirement to make the throne available to him.

25

GONE FISHING

One of the most interesting ways of spending a weekend was to go fishing with the locals, by dugout canoe. I had been working hard at my new job, putting in long hours and starting to see results. One Saturday morning, not long after my first arrival, I was greeted by a few of the fruit people who lived near the office.

"Would you like to go fishing with us tonight?"

I was delighted by the invitation and agreed without hesitation. "We will meet here at the railway track this evening at seven." This was the first of many invitations, which I always happily accepted if I could.

We met as arranged, at the railway line in front of the office, close to the foot of my knoll. Six men joined me, and we took one of the service rail cars to the end of the line, not very far from where the bus had dropped me off on the day I first arrived. A few more men were waiting for us there, as well as a small dugout canoe, belonging to one of them. Taking it in turns, four at a time, we had to carry the canoe on our shoulders. We had a fairly long walk from the edge of the farm to a small river, which flowed through the farm and met the sea at the end of a beach. This was the same river that passed the foot of my knoll, winding behind the office and through the bananas. It was also the river in which I occasionally swam. The dugout now made itself useful as it carried us, instead of us carrying it. Although a little over-loaded, we paddled gently down the river estuary towards the sea. Where the river met the beach we approached a small bamboo hut, partially hidden amongst the trees at the edge of the sand. The hut became our camp for the night. The first job, once we had unloaded the canoe, was to build a fire. Once this had been done we rested for a while, brewed a little coffee and then got down to the more important job of the night. We had to catch enough shrimps to bait the next morning's hooks. This was down by pushing a net, built like a scoop so that the leading edge scraped along the sand in the shallow water. The sand will sift through the net but the prawns or shrimps, and sometimes crabs will be caught. The prawn catching took a long time and was very tiring, as it required walking along the shore in knee-deep water, pushing this rather cumbersome net on a pole through the sand. Finally, well into the night, there was general agreement that we had caught enough. We were able to return to the hut, where the fire was a welcome focal point for weary fishermen.

We gratefully sat in the sand under a brilliant starlit night sky, relaxed and warmed ourselves after the long trek in the sea. The fire also gave us enough light to drink our coffee and eat some food that we had brought with us. Someone had a guitar and plucked out some local melodies, with some vocal accompaniment from the lads; so the hours passed swiftly and pleasantly. There was a bright crescent noon later, rising up from the sea, setting the scene for a very Brazilian night. Those who wished to could catch a little sleep, though most preferred to savour the passing of the perfect tropical night, amidst good friends and free from the daily toil of farm work. As the very first rays of light started to lift the darkness of the night, the atmosphere suddenly became one of purpose. The men went about their tasks with quiet efficiency, hardly uttering a word, as if any noise now might scare the fish away. The canoes were loaded, dragged down to the waters edge. The canoes we used for fishing kept permanently at the beach, hidden amongst the trees. The canoe that we had carried from the farm was in fact much smaller than the others; its job was merely to carry us along the short stretch of river from the road to the beach. The fire was carefully extinguished. The equipment that would not be taken in the canoes was hidden in some undergrowth near the hut. When all was ready we pushed our canoes out into the sea and paddled towards the breakers. There were usually four men to a boat and sometimes up to five boats. Those first few minutes were crucial, as we had to get beyond the breakers without mishap. It was important to take each breaker directly on the bows; the wrong angle could cause the boat to be rolled over by the waves. These canoes did not have outriggers. The sea was usually quite calm at this time in the morning unless there was a storm brewing so the breakers were quite small but we still had to be careful.

"Keep it steady," Alberto reminded us, as we headed our craft into the first of the breakers. "Once the wave lifts us we have to paddle fast." He was aiming his comments at me, as the others were experienced fishermen.

"I am ready," I reassured him.

We watched as the first wave lifted the bows. If we did not paddle through it, it would take us back to the beach.

"Right! Paddle as fast as you can," Alberto shouted over the sound of the wave breaking around us.

We all put our backs into it until we were safely beyond the wave. We had no time to celebrate, as the next wave was just yards away. We repeated the manoeuvre for each wave until we were beyond the breakers into calmer water. Once the breakers had been crossed, the sea was often almost glassy calm, except for the gentle rollers, lifting us and lowering us rhythmically, as we paddled out to meet the dawn.

Each canoe was laboriously cut out of a single tree trunk by hand. The men themselves had made the canoes, during many a weekend and evening. The canoes were wide enough for one man to sit quite comfortably as long as he sat low, otherwise they would be top heavy. They ranged from about twelve to eighteen feet and were surprisingly light. As we paddled out to sea, we stayed within sight of each other, although not too close and remained silent all the way. After paddling for about an hour, which took us a few miles from the beach, we anchored by throwing a stone tied to a long rope over the side—it was surprisingly shallow so far from the coast—and then we set about preparing our lines. The fishing tackle consisted of hand held lines, with a dead weight and a hook. The hooks were baited with the shrimps that we had laboriously caught in the nets the night before. We lowered the lines until they hit the bottom and then raised them slightly. Each boat was equipped with a large water-filled bucket for the fish, which soon started to fill as we began to see the fruits of our labours. The occasional splashing could be heard from the various boats, as fish were being caught though surprisingly not a sound from their usually highly vocal occupants. These men took their fishing very seriously. Even with my history of no luck with fishing, I was soon landing fair sized fish of all shapes and colours, some of which Alberto, or whoever was sharing the boat at the time, indicated with a hand signal, should be thrown back. I was usually able to make a reasonable contribution to the bucket. The most interesting fish I caught was a small hammerhead shark, about eighteen inches long.

We would stay out at sea until around noon, by which time the heat was unforgiving. I used to find that by late morning the smell of the now dried supply of shrimps and the fish, coupled with the continuous motion of the boat, was beginning to get to me. Even the occasional mouthful of the coffee we had brought was rapidly losing its effect. Although I enjoyed the excitement of catching the fish I had no complaint when the time came to call it a day. By the time we started home, the wind was usually blowing steadily and the sea was no longer the calm mill-pool of the early morning. I never found out who gave the signal but suddenly the boats would come alive, the anchors would be weighed and we would start paddling for the shore. As the boats closed in, the intense silence of the morning would be broken and there would be excited exchanges between the fishermen. Laughter filled the air as people exchanged stories, each telling of the one that got away or boasting of the size of their catch; all of which helped to pass the time during the long and far from easy pull for the shore.

Soon the sound of the breakers could be heard, and as we approached we could see the foam and spray lifted by the wind, as each wave curled under itself and hurled itself towards the shore. There was always a little nervousness as the tension built before we approached the breakers. The waves could get very big, and, if not handled carefully and with great skill, quite dangerous. None of us wanted to see our morning's work churned into the surf and liberated back into the sea. A wrong move or approaching the breaker from an angle could cause the very unstable canoe to roll. There was only one way to get to the shore and that was through the surf. There was always one experienced man in each boat who took charge and acted as helm as we approached our final hurdle. The helmsman would stand in the stern with a long paddle, and, while the rest of us paddled furiously on command, would steer the boat and give orders where necessary. At first the outer waves picked us up and eased us a little towards the shore before gliding silently past us, and then breaking ahead of us with a roar. The critical moment came when we were in the path of a wave just about to break. We paddled hard to gain momentum until we were picked up by the breaker and then our fate was in its hands. Once we were caught by the wave we shipped paddles and hopefully just enjoyed the ride.

For a frightening moment the canoe was picked bodily out of the water, and seemingly thrown towards the beach. A roll at this point could be very dangerous and if the wave was too high we could be slammed into the sandy bottom. We suddenly became engulfed in boiling foam, as we found ourselves surging madly towards the land. The foam subsided almost as fast as it had appeared, and after a few moments of more subdued motion we were gently touching the sand. The day's excitement was over. We now had the backbreaking job of hauling the canoes well above the high water mark, where they would be tethered awaiting the next outing. We then set about gathering the equipment as well as the precious fish. The long journey home, paddling against the stream back to the road and then carrying the canoe, was still ahead of us, before we could collapse into well-deserved sleep though not, of course, before sampling some of the fish.

It all served to remind one that it wasn't all that long ago that people had to go through similar ordeals for every meal they ate. There are in fact still many people who do just that.

26

MORE SURGERY, SOME REALTY SAVVY

The cattle herd of Sao Sebastioa was beginning to take shape; our new cows were calving and the milk yield was beginning to show signs of increasing. We received a present of two Red Poll bulls from Tres Barros to upgrade our herd. As we were gradually able to select a small nucleus of good, or at least reasonable, cows we could start to cross breed them with the Red Poll bulls. The goal was to eventually develop the same five eighth Red Poll cross as we were doing in Tres Barros. It would be many years before the breed would be fully recognized as the Pitangueiras and we were only just starting in Sao Sebastioa.

One of the bulls that we inherited was in fact a discard, on account of a large, football size tumour that had appeared on the side of his neck. We were only supposed to get the one bull but it was decided to send the other bull down to finish his days on light duty. It had been hinted that perhaps I would like to attempt a follow up on my udder operation, by removing the tumour, but I didn't take that idea too seriously. I had been lucky with the cow; however the word had got around, giving me a reputation bordering on rural legend, which I did not wish to have to live up to. Fate, however, took care of the arrangements.

A few weeks after the bulls had arrived, the one with the huge tumour started having trouble breathing. It appeared that the tumour was pressing on the trachea and the poor animal was suffering as well as in a state of panic, as each breath was a struggle for him. I could not just stand by and watch the poor creature suffer, so I decided to do what I could for the animal—there really was nothing to lose as the bull's days were clearly numbered. When I got to the retiro the bull was still standing and was still able to breathe though with obvious difficulty; each breath was accompanied by a loud wheeze and sometimes a rattling sound. I examined the tumour as best I could and, to my inexperienced touch, it appeared to be isolated and hopefully not adherent to surrounding tissue. After consulting Mr. Braham and the local doctor, I decided to take the gamble and try to remove the tumour. The local doctor was as helpful as Doc Moreno, my friend in Pitangueiras had been. Probably against medical ethics, the doctor not only helped me with essential supplies but also lent me a copy of Gray's Anatomy—in English, luckily, as he had done some of his studies in Guy's Hospital in London—pointing out the important structures in the area that I would be working in.

We used the same open gauze anaesthesia that I had used on the cow; however it took longer to knock the old bull out. Finally he quietened down and I started the long process of trying to circumnavigate the tumour, tying off all the bleeders, dissecting away all other tissue. The part immediately below the skin was fairly easy though as I went deeper I found that the tissue was not separating so well. It was difficult to avoid the larger vessels. Progress was slow, I found that I was dissecting tissue, cut by small cut, studiously tying off the vessels or cauterising them with my red-hot irons.

After a long time I straightened up and surveyed the scene, I saw that the ether was nearly gone yet the tumour was far from removed. The heat in the rather confined barn that I was working in was oppressive; I was bathed in sweat, some of which was from nervous tension. I had only been able to free a small portion of the deeper surface of the tumour, and the going was getting more difficult all the time. Parts of the tumour were infiltrating other structures and it was obviously not the benign, encapsulated growth that I had envisioned from my examination. I dejectedly returned to the operation, trying to get as much done before the ether ran out. Then I came to the real snag. I was able to identify the main vessels of the neck and the trachea and oesophagus, and realized that the tumour was intertwined with them. I tried to cut the tumour away from the structures but found that I was unable to control the bleeding as I did so. I missed the main structures however the tumour was rich with blood vessels. Cutting into it, as I had to, proved to be more than my surgical skill could manage.

I fought desperately for a while but I knew I was losing my patient. During my volunteer work I had seen a patient die on the operating table. This was different, this was my patient and I knew that I was losing him. I experienced a feeling of total helplessness, as I battled against the odds, and knew that they were stacked against both me, and more importantly, my patient. The ether ran out and I was still a long way from completing the operation. The patient was bleeding uncontrollably. I tried to tie off but the blood was coming so fast that I was unable to locate the sources. I did not dare to cauterize, so close to the Carotid Artery. I could make out some of the nerves; the Vagus nerve was close to the Carotid and the nerves of the neck, so I had little choice but to try to close up, knowing that I had failed. Very soon the bull would start to wake up. I had to make a quick decision.

At this point the surgeon-in-me was replaced by the farmer-in-me. I raised the scalpel once more, this time in the reluctant role of executioner. I had one advantage over the Mato Grosso fazenda butcher; he had to guess where the Carotid Artery was whereas I could see it as plain as day. After fighting to save my patient's life for so long, I had to steel myself to make the final incision. There was a sudden gush of rich red blood, contrasting sharply with the venous blood that filled the wound. As life was being pumped out onto the floor by the heart of the animal I had tried so hard to save, I had to turn away to hide the tears that were welling up in my eyes. I busied myself with clearing up the instruments and then gave instructions for the bull to be butchered. I rode sadly back to the house, where I stood under a shower for a full twenty minutes before I flopped onto the bed exhausted, mentally more than physically.

My cattle division office was in fact just an empty house in a row of workers' houses. It was simply furnished with two desks and two chairs and an old filing cabinet. I hired a young clerk to try to get some sort of index system going, and to keep track of the cows and calves, as well as the normal daily bookwork. It was all very informal and, being just part of the workers' lines, wives and children would wander in, or around the office, mainly just out of curiosity. I was, for a while at least, a local attraction, and would look up from my desk sometimes to find myself being stared at by a wide-eyed child. 'Familiarity breeds contempt' or so they say and I had become a familiar figure.

I was riding towards the office one day when I passed a rather buxom young mother breast-feeding her child. She looked up and saw me looking in her direction. We locked eyes for a moment and then with a cheeky grin she lifted the exposed breast and said "Quero mama?" (Would you like to drink?) I drew Pegasus in and started to dismount, calling her bluff. Thank heavens she did not call mine, instead scampered giggling back into the house with the baby under her arm. The peasant mother does breast-feed her child for quite a long time and children at the toddler stage and beyond are still offered the teat, more for reassurance than for sustenance. I had acquired a large calendar from somewhere, with a well-endowed Brazilian wench revealing all, and had it hanging above my desk. One day a small child wandered into the office and on seeing the calendar, stopped, looked longingly and then started to drool. I think he had suckling in mind, if not then he was a very precocious child.

One day when visiting a retiro in Mato Grosso, I had noticed that the retireiro's son was not helping his father as he usually was. This boy was about fourteen and being the only literate member of the family, was able to keep the books, as well as being a very good cowboy. We needed some figures, so I asked after the boy only to find that he was sick in bed. The retireiro took me in to see him. I was shocked to find that this rugged, handsome young cowboy, who would surely have been admired by his peers as the tough guy on any block, was lying in bed with a dummy in his mouth. The dummy had originally been red but was now black with age. It explained the black stain on the boy's front teeth that I had taken to be from smoking or chewing tobacco. I was to notice this similar stain on quite a number of youngsters' teeth; many of them went rotten.

Mr. Braham called me over to the office one day and introduced me to a gentleman, who had just driven down from Sao Paulo to view a piece of land he had bought. He had got it quite cheap and was quite pleased with his bargain. The salesman had told him that it would be an ideal spot for a weekend house as it was near the sea and had a spectacular view. We all studied the gentleman's map and compared it to one of our own, until the proud landowner was able to point out the exact location of his plot. I was just about to say something, when Mr. Braham, with a charming smile, suggested that I took the Paulista (person from Sao Paulo) to see the land he had bought.

"Why don't you take my rail car out to the border where our friend will have a clear view of the land he has bought?" The smile had a hint of mischief and I got the message loud and clear.

Following my boss's example I donned my best used-car-salesman smile and led the good gentleman out to the manager's rail car, which had a driver so Mr. Braham was confident that he would get it back in one piece. We spent the twenty minutes in pleasant conversation. The Paulista was clearly a city boy, as he asked me about the passing countryside as if it was his first time out of the Sao Paulo. The little car took us out to the far end of the farm, right in under the shadow of the mountains. Checking once more with the map, I pointed almost vertically at a peak, beyond even the highest of our hill pastures; even King Ludwig II of Bavaria would have thought twice about building one of his castles up there. There was no road or even footpath access; the salesman had been dead right about one thing, the view would have been fantastic.

I don't think we exchanged a single word on the way back, although I did detect a slight muttering under the breath but then it could have just been the wheels vibrating on the track. We never saw our landowner again; however I made one resolution that day, that I would never buy land unless I had put my feet on it first.

27

THE FARMS MANAGER PAYS ME A VISIT

Mr. Braham had also told me whilst I had been in his office, that a cable had just arrived to say that the Farms Manager, Roddy Taylor, was coming down for a visit. He had specifically asked to stay with me, rather than at the manager's house, which would have been the norm. With the knowledge that my ultimate boss was arriving, I had just a few days to get my house in order as well as my farm. I had a lot to do and very little time if I was going to make any sort of impression. I had had very little personal dealing with Roddy up to this point. He had visited the other farms, especially Tres Barros, which he took great interest in. I had shown him a few things at his request, especially on one occasion when DP had been away on vacation. My impression during those brief encounters had been that was he not very approachable and had looked on me as being far too junior to engage in conversation. Before coming down to Sao Sebastiao I had had quite a long conversation with him about what he had in mind for Sao Sebastiao but you don't really get to know a man during a business conference. I now had the somewhat daunting job of entertaining him, one on one for a few days and spending each day with him going round every inch of the farm. I had been sending reports regularly but now Roddy wanted to see for himself.

The first day was rather heavy going; this was the Roddy that I had known on previous occasions. I got the distinct impression that he was looking for faults. That evening, after we had retired to my mountain retreat, we discussed the day's inspection. To my considerable surprise and delight, Roddy expressed pleasure with what he had seen. He even complimented me on having achieved so much in the short time I had been there. The next day I felt more relaxed and realized that I had obviously imagined the tension and fault finding of the previous day. I gained a lot of good information and also useful advice from Roddy, and I could see why he was the Farms Manager. He was a great teacher once he came out of his shell, and he could also map out the future of the herd, thinking in terms of years and many generations of breeding. Roddy wanted to carry on the work of Tres Barros here in Sao Sebastiao, fixing a five eighth Red Poll/Zebu cross.

On the last day after lunch, Roddy declared a holiday and suggested that I take him to the beach for a little R&R. We spent the remainder of the day playing like two kids on the beach and in the surf. A couple of the workers from the farm were just coming back from a morning's fishing and allowed us to take their dugout that was still on the beach, back out to sea. With the workers watching with obvious amusement mixed with a little concern for the canoe, Roddy and I decided to try our luck at riding the moderate sized waves. Roddy was as excited as a school boy when we came crashing in on the crest of the wave, with me frantically trying to keep the thing pointing in the right direction. I dunked him once but after recovering the boat and baling it out, we were both game for another go. We were becoming more successful with each practice run.

My house was rather lonely that night after Roddy had left for Sao Paulo; the man I had feared had become a friend and I had enjoyed his company. The following day I was able to see my funny little straggly farm as being a part in the whole scheme of things. I felt distinctly superior to the rest of my local cattle colleagues who were only aware of Sao Sebastiao and its day-to-day events.

One of the sidelines on Sao Sebastiao was the sugar cane, which was used for making Pinga, known locally as Cachaça, a very popular local spirit that packed quite a punch. There was only a small area of land set aside for sugar but the company also bought sugar from the surrounding area. The Pinga factory was within the farm; close to the small banana loading pier and it produced a very good and well-respected brand of Pinga. I had first been introduced to Pinga on Tree Barros and I remember Frank, who very seldom drank hard liquor, starting innocently enough with a jug of Caipirinha, Pinga mixed with lemon and sugar, which was very palatable, and slowly drinking his way through it during one evening. We were at the Jarrold's (of alligator and vulture fame) house at the time. After dinner Frank was missing, only to be found out in the garden, empty jug cradled in his arms and his dinner, which had returned, being eaten by the dogs.

In the bars in Pitangueiras, as in any of the interior towns, the locals would come in for a quick pick-me-up of neat Pinga. It always amused me to see these men come in with a look of heightened anticipation and demand 'uma cachaça,' which meant a small glass of straight Pinga. With one sweep of the arm they would cause the liquid to disappear; their next move would be to hold on to the edge of the bar. The full force of the lethal stuff hit them within seconds with the classical head shaking, eye bulging, double take, as the men reeled from the shock. After holding on to the bar for a moment, as the man recovered from the first shock-wave, he would then demand "mais uma cachaça," and then repeat the entire performance before marching, a little guardedly, out into the street once more.

A similar ritual to the cachaça pick-me-up is re-enacted constantly throughout Brazil, with the cafezino, which is a small cup of very strong, black coffee with half the cup filled with the powdery sugar, peculiar to Brazil, which makes it sickly sweet. In all the major towns there are little cafezino bars at most corners, where people come in and down a cup in one mouthful, and return to the street within moments. It lacks the drama of the cachaça and is a very pleasant upper to help a person through the day.

One of my favourite excursions on the railcar at Sao Sebastiao was to the loading dock at Porto Novo, where the bananas were loaded onto the barges. The rails went out of the farm and through a neighbouring farm in the next valley, which belonged to Ademah de Barros. He had been the Governor of the State of Sao Paulo, however because of his involvement in a massive swindle, involving imported cars, he was exiled and, for some years lived in the States. Ademah was a great champion for the workingman and would often point at the foreign companies, accusing them of injustices towards the workers.

It was, to say the least, ironic to see the contrast between the foreign owned Sao Sebastiao and Ademah de Barros' farm, where the workers were housed in very substandard houses, little more than shacks, and paid the lowest wages in the area. We often had Ademah's workers coming to Sao Sebastiao applying for jobs but because Ademah was once more in office we did not dare to hire them.

How Ademah returned is one of those things that could only happen in South America. After Ademah had left, it had been stated that if he ever returned he would face criminal charges. The office for Prefeituro (Chief of Police) was an elected office. So the next election found Ademah de Barros standing for election for Prefeituro. Being a political candidate, he was able to return to Brazil. After a very high-powered election campaign Ademah was duly elected. Very soon after that of course, his police record mysteriously disappeared.

The Porto was a delightful spot. A fifteen-minute train ride beyond the farm boundary surrounded by lush and unspoiled tropical jungle. There was a wooden jetty for the river barges and a small warehouse. The Pinga factory was close by giving out a sweet odour of sugar. It was like a remote Amazon River trading station. The wooden jetty was situated about half a mile from the sea, up the Rio (river) Juqueryquera. As I stood there on the jetty watching them load the bananas, I almost expected to hear tribal drums accompanying the sad strains of Caribbean Calypsos. The mostly Negro workers, whose sweat streamed naked torsos glistened in the brilliant sunlight, each carrying one huge bunch of bananas, formed a human conveyor belt, running down a narrow plank to the waiting barges. I seldom, if ever, had a genuine excuse for going to Porto Novo, however I often invented one, just to experience the exotic Caribbean fantasy.

Pedro, Joao and me: working in the corral.

28

BARRETOS, THE WEIGH MASTER

I was beginning to settle down to the feeling of belonging. The Sao Sebastiao cattle section was becoming my own domain; it had started as just an idea and now it was a serious little dairy and breeding farm. I started a little gardening in my hilltop home and thought of ways to make my house a tad more comfortable. It was of course the lull before the storm. I had always spoken very highly of Joao Pereira and meant every word of it. The trouble was that the cattle section was a low priority and low budget affair. As soon as the groundwork was done the powers-that-be decided that it did not need an 'Ingles' to run the herd. Joao was made section manager, and I was packing my bags once more. This time I was off to Barretos, to run the cattle receiving and weighing yard for the meat factory as well as the Barretos fazenda. I had of course spent many a weekend at Barretos when DP and I had driven up from Pitangueiras and I still had the pleasant memories of my first boiada that ended there.

    I hated to leave Sao Sebastiao. I left a lot of myself in that little valley and yet I looked bravely to the future and fought back a tear as Lindy and I were driven out of the farm to meet the bus at Caraguatatuba.

    After one night in the Sao Paulo, staying with Roddy, who kindly agreed to let Lindy stay in my room with me, I once more boarded the night train that had first taken me to Tres Barros. This time I would go a little further to Barretos. I was retracing the same route I had taken on my first plunge into the interior of

Brazil, almost two years before. I was a very different person to the green horn fresh from England who had been met by DP in Pitangueiras. After a good night's sleep, lulled by the rhythmic tattoo of wheels on rail ends, I woke early enough to be able to pop my head out of the window, as we stopped at Pitangueiras. I had just a brief glimpse of the little town I had got to know. There was the familiar town square in front of the church, where we had watched the town's singles talent, of both sexes, parading on Saturday evenings. Across the square I could just see the club, the social centre of the swinging set. I was able to get a little more sleep and then a leisurely breakfast before arriving at Barretos.

Lindy was now nearly fully grown. A large Alsatian was hardly the best animal for a bachelor's room at the Barretos factory mess. I was a little worried in case somebody said "no dogs" however the subject was never even discussed. Lindy and I were able to settle down quite happily amongst many familiar faces, as well as enjoy all the social whirl of the Barretos community. It could only be likened to a sergeant's mess with all the rank consciousness and social climbing that goes along with it.

I had to adjust myself to a new discipline. I had been used to creating something new, and now I had to fit into a well-established, well-oiled routine, governed by the factory's insatiable appetite for meat and the constant arrival of cattle to feed it. I still had a farm to run but any farming had to be done between the arrivals of the boiadas. The receiving corrals and weighing room became my second home. As I watched batch after batch of identical steers being herded into the balance, doomed for the slaughterer's sledgehammer, I longed for Sao Sebastiao and my own little herd.

I soon became part of the Barretos scenery however and immersed myself into my new job. The cattleman is always the oddball at the factory, because he doesn't really come under the factory management and yet lives in symbiosis with the community. He is merely attached and therefore it is difficult for anyone to fit him into a convenient slot, when it comes to seniority, which is so important to people who live in these tight company communities.

I had seen a similar situation in Abadan, Iran, in the oil refinery. My stepfather had been posted there as manager for BOAC for a while. There the oil company people were conveniently housed in 'A, B or C' houses, according to the rank of the employee. 'A' house people would not mix with 'B' house people, and when a man got promotion into the section above, he had to change his friends. It wasn't quite so bad at Barretos although there was always the feeling of rank and position, most noticeable at the club. Little groups of equals would segregate themselves from lesser, or greater equals. Gossip was of course the daily fare and nobody escaped the coffee time laparotomy, or that awful feeling as you come into the bar and the conversation suddenly changes. You are quite certain that you have been the topic of discussion up to that point. On the whole I was able to get on with my job in the reception corral, or on the farm and seldom come into contact with the factory people in my official capacity.

From time to time I would go up onto the killing floor, not for any morbid curiosity but to learn about cattle. I would see the cattle coming into the corral and get a general impression of the animals, I would then weigh them estimating the dead weight—there was a formula for this; it varied according to the size of animal and age, as well as the build. By following the animals up to the killing floor I could see how far my estimates were out. I could see the amount of fat compared with lean, and the amount of bone. An actual dead weight was calculated after slaughter and it was interesting to compare the actual dead weight with the estimated weight whilst in-vivo. Weighing is not an exact science, as one has to try to bend a little, to get the most accurate formula for each type of animal. I was constantly trying to be fair to both the factory and the farmer, who is selling the cattle and being paid on my calculation. Many an argument could erupt over the outcome and I did not cherish the idea of being on the wrong end of an argument with a gun toting Latin cowboy with an attitude.

After I had been at the factory for a few months, there was an annual cattle show held in the local town of Barretos. I was to be one of the officials, an honour bestowed on me due to my position as official receiver and weigher for the Anglo factory. The show was held on the other side of town where, for some reason that I never determined, there was a large cattle scale similar to ours. My first job on arriving very early in the morning was to calibrate the scale; with the cage empty I had to adjust the scale until it read zero. One of the main attractions for the local cattlemen was a steer competition. Each competitor had to enter a batch of ten steers. They were judged as a group and so had to be as uniform as possible. We weighed the cattle in the early morning, so that the weights were available later during the judging. There was keen competition amongst the local farmers, which meant that the calculations were keenly scrutinized and hotly contested. There would be great emotion if they thought I had under estimated their animals, of if they did not agree with the gross weight. On one occasion we had to clear the animals out of the scale and recalibrate just to satisfy one very suspicious farmer.

The annual occasion was a true cattleman's affair. The crowd-pleasing rodeos took centre stage for most of the morning. Another point of interest was the ever-popular calf lassoing and roping. It was all good fun although taken very seriously by the local population. Saddles, sheepskins, wide brimmed hats, capes and knee length boots were being bought and sold in the many stalls around the competition arenas. The delicious smell of barbecued meat permeated the hot dusty air. At one point I was standing watching the fun when I noticed, next to me, one of the most rugged, craggy faced cowboys I had ever seen. He was resplendent in finery, a huge gun in his belt and a sharp skinning knife tucked into the back of his belt, as was the custom. At the moment my eyes met his, his hand was just reaching his mouth holding a Popsicle ice cream. The rugged cowboy image was shattered.

Later that morning the steers were paraded before the judges, groomed to perfection and led proudly round the ring for all to admire. The Grand Finals of this particular event took place away from the madding crowd, in the somewhat sinister surroundings of the Anglo Factory killing floor. I remember being somewhat surprised at the apparent affection shown by the farmers towards their steers as they had led them round the judging ring, and their lack of emotion as they watched them being bludgeoned to death. The same men who had lovingly patted their prize animals now proudly escorted them along the conveyor belt, watching with that same proud affection, as their animals were slowly reduced to sides of grade 'A' beef. What had started out as a beautiful day in the sun, with the animals looking their best for the occasion had ended for them as it had for the Jews at Dachau. Cattle shows have never really attracted me since then.

One of my perks as cattleman at Barretos was my camionette, which I required for getting around the farm. The vehicle was a definite asset towards my popularity amongst the bachelors, ensuring an invitation to anywhere that required transport. This could range from the Red light district, to more distant journeys around the Barretos area. There were several of the company farms within driving distance of the factory. Many were the weekends that a camionette load of Barretos bachelors would head off for lunch and tennis, at a farm as far as a hundred kilometres away. On one of those occasions, having spent the day on one of the farms, we passed through a small town and stopped for a drink. We found that there was a dance going on in a building across the street. We joined the dance for a while but having ordered and consumed only a couple of rounds of drinks, we found the local girls somewhat standoffish, refusing even to talk to us, let alone dance with us. We left the dancehall and decided to have just one more drink for the road at the small bar across the street.

Whilst we were sitting at the bar the telephone rang, and being a little merry, I facetiously said to the barman as he answered it, "If that's for me tell them I'm out".

The barman listened for a moment as the caller said something, and then without a flicker of a smile, he handed it to me and said, "It's for you."

Apparently we had left the dance without paying for one of the rounds of drinks and had been seen to go into the bar. After getting over the shock, and then our laughter, we returned to the dancehall and paid our bill.

One of the few times I have ever sent the wine back and refused the bottle, took place in a tiny roadside café in a remote village, somewhere between Barretos and one of the farms. We had stopped for dinner, ordered from the rather limited menu, and ordered a bottle of Brazilian wine to accompany the meal. When the wine came the waiter-cum proprietor pulled out the cork but half remained in the bottle; not as one piece however, more like grains of sand. The first glassful looked more like a fruit salad so we sent it back. The proprietor was rather put out yet disappeared behind the counter and hay-presto returned with a glassful of wine each. One taste was enough to detect his method, as the wine had a distinct dishcloth flavour; we ordered beer instead.

I was loading some seed sacks onto the camionette one day, to take to a replant pasture and dented the fender whilst backing the camionette. I soon found myself the center of a lot of teasing by the British factory personnel, all in fun and mainly in English. One of the factory drivers, hearing the laughter, came over to see what had happened. He became very angry when he saw what the joking was about and shouted at the jokers, saying in essence that people who worked hard were bound to have accidents. I remember his words to this day "Quem Trabalho batte mesmo," though what impressed me most was the fact that he had felt such a fierce loyalty towards another driver, regardless of race or rank, and had come to my defence.

I received a letter from my mother to say that she was on her way to Montevideo to join my stepfather, who was with BOAC there. The airline was preparing to open up the South American route again after a few years of suspension, though they had not started flights yet. My mother was therefore going down to join him by ship. As her ship was to call at both Rio de Janeiro and Santos, she suggested that I should try to come down to either one or the other ports, so that we could have at least a few hours together whilst the ship was docked. The ship my mother was travelling on was one of the Vesteys' ships, the Paraguay Star from their Blue Star line, so I enquired through Sao Paulo whether I could be given a couple of days leave and also whether they could get a berth on the ship from Rio to Santos. Happily head office complied with both my requests.

When the day arrived I set off once more for Sao Paulo. I was entitled to one night's hotel in Sao Paulo, as I was going to report to the office; however the trip to Rio and the hotel was to be on my account. When I arrived in Rio, I asked the taxi driver to take me to a hotel. I didn't know the names of any except for one where the BOAC crews used to stay when I had been in Rio visiting my mother and stepfather many years before, so I suggested that one.

We arrived at the hotel with a flourish, minions were eagerly grabbing my bags—well one small, rather scruffy canvas bag; they search for the rest until they realized that that was the rest—while a liveried doorman was hovering around shouting orders and opening the door for me. The new arrival and his entourage converged on the reception desk. Seeing the obvious splendour and extravagance of the hotel foyer, I started to get the impression that I had chosen a slightly more expensive hotel that I had bargained for. I asked whether they had a room, hoping that they would say no, instead the receptionist smiled happily and assured me that they did. Out came the inevitable form and guest book. A pen was gently thrust into my now trembling hand. Panic overtook me at this point; I could see myself having to wash the chandeliers for months, to pay for all this. I laid down the pen and asked very sheepishly, "how much for one night?" Now my salary, on the farm was "all found", so that while I was on the farm I wanted for nothing. I had accommodation, food and servants, as well as transport. My salary was just enough to cover those little extras, like clothing, the occasional drink and modest night out. This was regular practice on the farms, so that once off the farm we were paupers to be pitied; however I expected and certainly got no pity from the hotel reception clerk. The price he quoted was about half my monthly salary and that didn't include tax, tips and the evening's meal. I did some quick leadership-potential thinking, and asked whether Lloyd George had booked in already. The clerk looked through the book and to my profound relief said "Not yet Sir".

"Ah" I replied, "I had better wait before booking in, he said he would probably be here, if not he would be at the Hotel Cruzeiro," which I had noticed across the street.

Leaving my suitcase I walked out in the direction of the Cruzeiro although I actually walked on by. I walked for quite a while before coming to a less prosperous part of the town, and after enquiring from a few people, was able to locate a small pension; where the rooms were awful but the price was right. I booked a room and returned to the hotel to collect my luggage. Not wanting to further the intrigue with any more lies, I merely collected my suitcase without any explanation and returned to the pension. The proprietor was a burly looking woman, who demanded the night's rent in advance and led me to my room; well room is crediting it with a little more dignity than it possessed. My cubicle was barely large enough to house the bed and leave room to manoeuvre; however it was a place to sleep, which was all I needed. I had slept in a lot worse up country, so I was quite content. I had the remainder of the day to rediscover the beautiful city of Rio de Janeiro.

Rio is a city of variety and character, unlike Sao Paulo, which is just another big concrete jungle. Rio was a gem set in an azure blue sea, fringed with some of the world's most spectacular beaches and backed by the high pinnacles of mountains pointing high into the sky. The town itself is a mixture of the old and the new, of extravagant luxury and abject poverty. The foothills were covered with flavellas, which are small shacks, made of whatever is available and inhabited by a mixed population; although a higher percentage are Negro or part Negro. I had, some years previously, spent many a day walking up through these flavellas and seeing the conditions that the people lived in.

There was a hospital that I recognized, where my mother had done some volunteer work during the four years she and my stepfather were posted there. The hospital was run by a missionary, specially for the children of the flavellas, who were suffering from severe malnutrition. I had been horrified to see these poor little children, with limbs withered down to the bone, bellies bloated and eyes sunken into the skull. They had faces of the aged; wrinkled, hollow-eyed and apathetic, beyond suffering. As a rule these starving children were more the result of ignorance, as there were places in Rio where mothers could go to seek help. In many cases the parents were not starving yet somehow they just neglected the children or fed them with very dilute powdered milk, to save money.

Now that I could speak Portuguese, I returned to the flavellas and spent part of the afternoon just chatting to the people there. I got the impression that they were not really a very unhappy people; the air was filled with the sound of laughter and music, not just from a radio, but music hammered out by whatever means was available. Cleanly dressed, cheerful, smiling children were returning from school. The people I met did not seem to be embittered by their circumstances; they were busy and to some degree content making the best of the situation. Most of the children were going to school during the day and spending the evenings picking up some extra money by begging or shining shoes down in the city's streets; the luckier ones getting what part-time jobs they could find. Many of the houses were quite well built and comfortable inside. I sat down with one family and shared a pot of coffee with them. These people were as interested in me, and what I did, as I was in them and their lives. I was able to tell them about parts of their own country that they knew nothing about.

My next port of call was the Copacabana beach, where we had lived, or at least my parents had lived and I had visited on a school holiday. My means of transport was the tram. The single-decker trams were always full and one just had to hang on to the uprights, often three people deep. The conductor had to clamber over and around this mass of humans and somehow keep a track of who had paid and who had not. The famous beach was as busy and colourful as ever. The pavement, with its mosaic patterns, was still thronged by sun loving locals and tourists alike. I hadn't brought my swimwear, so I just strolled along the beach and watched the familiar sights. The inevitable football games were being played on the beach, bordered on one side by the pounding of the surf, and on the other by the string of huge hotels and apartment buildings that fronted the beach from end to end. I bought an ice cream from the Ku-bon man as he rode along the front on his bicycle. I walked into the Copacabana Palace Hotel and sat on the Terrace, ordered an iced coffee and just watched the world go by.

There were many restaurants along the front and sometimes my parents and I had come out for dinner, sitting out in the open, with just a low hedge or railing between our table and the street. On one occasion I had been sitting next to the fence, beyond which was a narrow hedge. From time to time the beggars from the flavellas would come and look over the fence and ask for money, not really expecting any. As I was sitting waiting for the meal to come, I felt a slight movement at my elbow, and, looking down, I saw my bread roll just disappearing through the hedge. I looked over the fence to find a small girl with large eyes, reminiscent of Margaret Keane's paintings, clutching the roll and looking at me with fear in her eyes. My first thought had been, on seeing her clutching the roll, how could she eat that without butter, so I reached down and passed her a pat of butter.

As I was enjoying the reminiscences, I noticed a group of Englishmen at a neighbouring table; they seemed to be having a problem with ordering a meal and in typical English style, when not understood, were repeating themselves with ever increasing decibels. They obviously knew no Portuguese and the waiter knew no English, so a definite impasse had been reached. I offered to help but was greeted at first with further confusion. Although I was speaking to them in English, they seemed to assume that I must be speaking in Portuguese and so did not understand me. After an awkward moment, it clicked and they were delighted to accept my help. They were out in Rio for a short time installing some major piece of refrigerating machinery. We ended up spending the evening together.

As this was the Englishmen's second night in Rio, they were experts on the local nightlife and led me to one of the nightclubs. We were greeted on our arrival, by a scantily clad but irate hostess, who accosted us loudly, hurling abuse at one of the men. He of course did not speak a word of Portuguese, so it fell to me to interpret. It transpired that the man had taken the girl to his hotel the night before and had then refused to pay her for her services. A long discussion ensued, the outcome of which, surprisingly enough was that they would repeat the deal that night with the proviso that he would pay in advance. I became fascinated by the belly dancer and after her gyrations on stage we invited her over to the table. She was very good company and I was getting along well with her. She later suggested going to her place but when we came down to terms, she was way out of my league. We nevertheless spent a happy and enjoyable evening together and parted as friends.

I left my friend at the Copacabana Palace and returned to my modest, or should I say frugal abode and slept late the next morning. I still had plenty of time before the ship was to dock. I lunched in a nearby restaurant and had the best 'fejuada completa' I had ever had. This is a meal made up of pig's intestines, ears, trotters and the peasants' staple, black beans and rice. It is the poor man's feast in the interior. I had enjoyed a few 'fejuadas' up country, however this one was superb.

My mother's ship was due to arrive in the early afternoon and I was eager to see her, so I made my way down to the docks. The ship was due to stay in Rio for a few hours before leaving for Santos. I found myself at the same dock where my ship, the Debrett, had berthed, what seemed like years ago, but was only two and a half years. When I found the ship, The Paraguay Star, she was already alongside preparing to make fast. My mother was delighted to see me and even more so when she heard that I was booked to travel on the ship to Santos. We spent the few hours in Rio looking at the old haunts, much as I had been doing myself over the previous twenty-four hours. We returned to the building where we had lived and were able to locate a few of the old friends but as it had been quite a few years since we had lived there many people had moved on. We had a pleasant journey down to Santos. I was able to catch up on all the family gossip. We talked deep into the night, each eager to hear the other's news, neither wanting to waste the talking time on sleep; finally we were both exhausted and reluctantly turned in for the remainder of the night.

When I awoke the following morning I immediately sensed the lack of rhythmic movement in the ship. The engine noise was gone, replaced by the alien sounds that indicate that a ship is no longer a self-sufficient echo-system; she is now just another freighter alongside the jetty. We had arrived at Santos; my all-too-short cruise was over. We still had a few hours before the ship sailed, so my mother and I were able to breakfast leisurely and spend a little time ashore before we had to bid each other farewell once more and return to our own very different lives: my mother back to a passenger ship, bound for Montevideo, where she would be caught up in the social whirl as wife of the BOAC manager, for me, it was back to the interior of Brazil, and although I did not know it at the time, soon to be sent from Barretos up to one of the big fattening farms in the North West of the State of Sao Paulo.

Roddy Taylor broke the news of my next posting as he passed through Barretos a few weeks later. He had been at one of the other farms in the area and spent a night in Barretos before returning to Sao Paulo. He asked me if I would take him to the airport to catch his flight. As we drove through the town of Barretos towards the airport he told me that I was to start winding up and get ready to transfer to Jacaracatinga.

We stood on the tarmac watching Roddy's plane arrive; those were the days of very casual air travel. We were chatting as the passengers started to emerge from the plane. Suddenly there was a scream of delight, as a rather over dressed lady passenger emerged. She was looking and waving at us. It must have been us as there was no one else close by. As she reached the tarmac she ran towards us, arms outstretched. In a moment of horror I recognized her as the 'Madame' of our favourite 'house'; we used to call her 'The Judge'. I braced myself for an embarrassing encounter and the necessary explanations, when she ran straight past me and threw herself into Roddy's arms. Just as I was getting used to the change in events she reach over and patted my cheek.

"She hasn't changed a bit," said Roddy as the 'Judge' headed off for the airport building. "Always cheerful."

"Yes, she's always good fun." I managed to regain enough voice to reply.

I watched Roddy's plane leave with a heavy heart. Not because Roddy was leaving but because of the news he had just broken to me. I was very content with my present job and enjoyed the very social life of Barretos; however it was more about my next manager that had caused my heart to sink. Pearman had a very bad reputation amongst the assistants.

29

JACARACATINGA, MY NEMESIS

When it came time to packing up once more, I really only had one personal regret. I had in the previous few months become particularly attracted to Wendy, a part Chinese girl from Barretos. I had met her at various dances and had occasionally invited her to come to the Club to swim, or play tennis. At first it had developed as no more than a friendship. Like most of my bachelor colleagues, I had become rather wary of deep romantic involvements in Brazil, so most of our womanising was done in the Red Light area, where there was no danger of becoming emotionally involved. The local girls we met at the dances always came equipped with built in chaperones, and so we had no choice but to behave. If it did appear to the family that a young man was getting more than a little interested in the daughter, he was either given the treatment and sent packing, or worse still, he was looked upon as an eligible contender for the marriage stakes. If this happened he virtually became their property. For some reason the Ingles bachelors from the farms were particularly favoured. The locals had the idea that we were rich young fazendeiros, with good prospects. If this happened then you were in trouble, as you found yourself having to escort the girl everywhere, and if you so much as looked at another girl, it was taken as an insult to the entire family. To be seen to lead a girl on and then dump her was calling for serious trouble, especially if there had been even a hint of sex. One poor misguided bachelor had

had to quit and leave Brazil for fear of the wrath of the brothers of his girlfriend after they had been caught alone and in a state of inappropriate undress.

Wendy seemed to have more freedom than the others, which allowed for a more relaxed friendship. At first she was always with her group of friends but gradually she preferred to meet me alone. On my last night before leaving for Jacaracatinga, we went to a dance together in Barretos. There was quite a large group of us from the factory though Wendy and I found every excuse we could to drift away from the rest of the party. We spent most of the evening locked together in the middle of the dance floor, oblivious to the rest of the world. After the dance had finished we walked the streets of Barretos trying to prolong the hour of parting. Finally at her door we could compose ourselves no longer and with tears rolling down our cheeks, lips found lips as passion overcame prudence.

Jacaracatinga, situated one hundred kilometres out from Aracatuba, was one of the largest of the company's fattening farms. It was well formed, with the best grasses and efficient, well-controlled retiros. I had, so far, been on all the farms with a difference. The two dairy farms were both mixed, one with citrus and the other with bananas and one small fattening farm was adjacent to the Barretos factory. The Mato Grosso farms, although purely for cattle, could not be regarded as typical, or indeed as fattening farms. Now I was going to one of the many pure fattening farms, which were the main business of the company. Jacaracatinga was, strictly speaking also mixed, as the company owned a large coffee estate adjacent to although completely separate from the cattle land. Unlike both Tres Barros and Sao Sebastiao, where there was one manager over both the fruit and the cattle divisions, the coffee estate of Jacaracatinga was administered completely separately under Mr. Ederley the manager with three English assistants.

After being met at the airport by the driver and a three-hour drive from Aracatuba; I approached Jacaracatinga with serious mixed feelings. I was glad to be back on the farms again; despite the pleasant social life in Barretos, the day-to-day job was mostly confined to the factory, with little time to farm. I had enjoyed the life in Barretos yet I had felt that I was standing still and not getting on with the business of learning to be a farmer. As I mentioned, my reason for not being entirely glad about my new posting, was the manager, Mr. Pearman, who had a reputation for being a very unpleasant person and not being very easy to work for. My only sign of welcome on arriving on the farm came from the Ederleys and a few of the other coffee people, which was the sign of things to come. I did not meet Pearman until the following day. I had arrived at the office, where I had been met by the clerk and was sitting at my allotted desk looking through the latest stock reports. Lindy, my now fully-grown Alsatian, was lying quietly on the floor by my side. I heard a vehicle draw up outside, moments later the door swung open and a tall handsome man, not unlike an enlarged David Niven, walked in. I stood up ready to introduce myself but he walked past without seeming to notice me and called the clerk in. I sat for a while whilst Pearman and the clerk discussed some routine points. The clerk came out and resumed his seat. I continued to sit at my desk, waiting until finally Pearman deigned to remember me some ten minutes later. He called me in.

"You're Vaughan," he informed me, which incidentally I already knew. "I don't want to see your dog in the office. Either leave her at home or outside the office."

I deferred to his order and waited for the interview to start.

"I will let you know if I want you to do anything, meanwhile don't do anything." He lowered his eyes to the paper work in front of him and I assumed that the meeting was over.

I walked back to my new house, which was very near the office, somewhat crest-fallen and far from delighted with my first encounter with the infamous Pearman. The housekeeper greeted me kindly and made me some breakfast. I spent the rest of the day unpacking my things, and getting to know my new home and garden. The house was a very pleasant bungalow with a large garden that had clearly been well looked after in the past. The view from the house was of an endless expanse of pasture, dotted with cattle. As I walked around the garden the sight of some old friends cheered me a little; there were some orange trees, a few bananas and some papayas, known in Brazil as 'mamao'.

A huge bougainvillea formed an arch leading to the front door. I noticed a chicken run in the back, which I later stocked and became quite a chicken farmer. That was later, now I had to face an uncertain future with a very unpleasant boss.

I suppose I had been lucky up to this point; I had been working in situations where, except for the very early days, I had automatically assumed responsibility and was allowed to decide my own working hours and methods. I had always willingly put in long hours and enjoyed taking responsibility. It was therefore difficult for me to adapt to a way of life where I had to wait for orders and find that I was being given little jobs to do that any fifteen-year-old peasant could have done. I found that instead of being able to get going in the morning and get out into the farm, I had to wait at the office until Pearman arrived, which was about nine o-clock, so that half the day was wasted. I was then routinely sent on useless missions.

One day's orders that I remember vividly, illustrate the stupidity of the man. Pearman had arrived as usual, sweeping through the office without so much as a nod of acknowledgement to my polite "Good morning Sir." I sat in anticipation for the mandatory half an hour during which he ignored me. Finally he called me in and told to me to check on the ploughing for the new planting, then find out if one of the retiros had finished a pig enclosure that they were working on, and finally check on some workers replacing a damaged stretch of fence. "Eureka! Responsibility."

My mode of transport was by horse and so I planned my route so as to be able to cover all three places within the day. It was quite a ride to cover all three places so I lost no time dawdling.

As I arrived at the ploughing, I spotted Pearman's blue cruiser just leaving from the other end of the field. When I got to the pig enclosure, the retireiro was surprised to see me because he informed me "Senhor Pearman just left here an hour ago."

I knew that a visit to the fence workers was a waste of time, as Pearman had probably been there already. Nevertheless I soldiered on knowing that he would probably ask me some trick question to prove that I had not gone there. What a complete waste of a day that was.

It took a long time before I was able to acquire any real responsibility, a lot of which I just went out and did, consequences be damned. If I had been learning something during this time, it would not have been too bad although I really felt that I was being held back by the very man who should have been the one most interested in my desire to learn.

Pearman was an insecure man, who trusted no one and reaped the harvest that he had sown. He was hated by the local farm workers, who would cheat him if and when they could. I had become used to trusting the people on the farms and very seldom came across real dishonesty amongst the locals. It was foreign for me to have to check up on every little thing and suspect every one of cheating me. This became quite a bone of contention between Pearman and me. He of course took it as being proof of my laziness.

On a very few occasions during my stay on Jacaracatinga, I was invited to the Pearmans' house, usually when a company official was visiting. Pearman would be the perfect host, as he greeted me with a dashing smile, treating me like a beloved son in front of the guests. The following morning I was well advised to stay as far clear of him as I could. He would treat me with even greater contempt and look for excuses to humiliate me, just to make sure that I did not take advantage of his staged friendship of the previous night.

Away from Pearman, I enjoyed Jacaracatinga. It was a beautiful farm, with clean pastures, well stocked with good grass and fat healthy cattle—many of which had probably passed through my hands in Mato Grosso. It was a joy to ride through pastures and be able to see hundreds of almost identical cattle, clean, healthy and contented, in almost ideal surroundings. There was no commitiva like we had in Ligacao, as each retiro looked after its own cattle. The retiros had their own team of men, which included foot-workers, as well as horsemen. Each retiro was in essence a complete farm. Obviously when a lot of men were required in one part of the farm, we would call in men from other retiros.

As I had no great responsibility, I was at least free during the day to ride around the retiros and get to know the retireiros and their crews, as well as the pastures, fences, waterholes and of course the cattle. The farm was shaped like a pear, with the sede at the narrow end. A fairly wide and fast flowing river formed the border on one side the farm, and on the other there was a long strip of forest; although belonging to the farm it was left as woodland and not used for grazing. There was always a good deal of replanting going on, so I would spend some time there; often relieving the tractor driver and happily ploughing for an hour or so.

Sometimes I would notice that a fence did not appear on the map, or that it differed from the map. I would do some surveying and plot the fence on the map. This was done by various methods. The old-faithful chain was used to measure a distance and the angles were measured with a rather primitive transit, which was little more than a compass with a sight. In some of the replanting areas contour ditches were needed to reduce erosion during the various stages of the replant. I became quite expert at doing the contouring. We did this with a long plastic tube filled with water, mounted at either end on an extendable, graded wooden pole. Each operator could read the level of the water in the tube, which, when two poles of equal length are placed on the same plain, should be equal. The distance between each contour level was determined with the same instrument. By extending one pole by the required amount, and then moving the pole slowly down the slope until the two water levels were equal. All this surveying required a lot of footwork but I found it fascinating and spent many days happily engaged plodding up and down the replants; at least it got me out of Pearman's hair. I had to get his permission to alter the map where I had found discrepancies, which he begrudgingly gave whilst grumbling about me wasting my time. Wasting time seemed to be my main purpose in life.

Once the area for replanting had been ploughed and contoured we would plant a cash crop: usually corn on the high land and rice on the lower areas. Between the rows Coloniao grass would be planted in clumps fairly far apart.

Coloniao grass was the latest grass to be introduced to the pastures. It was a very coarse grass but if kept fairly short by grazing was a good feed. Coloniao seemed to weather the dry season better than previous grasses. The corn would grow quickly and would be ready to harvest by the time the grass had taken hold. After the corn had been harvested the stalks were bent over, so that the grass would have the benefit of the sunshine and thus be allowed to come to seed. We would then put some cattle into the area for a few days at this juncture, so as to scatter the seeds and get them trampled into the soil.

When the cattle had been removed the whole replant area would be burnt. This was to clear the corn stumps, as well as the long Coloniao grass, which, when it has grown to seed, is almost like bamboo and not a good feed. It is a very fast burn and a good percentage of the seeds survived, at least the ones that had been trodden into the ground. After the corn and grass have been burnt off it is left, to allow the seeds to grow. We tried to burn as near to the beginning of the wet season as possible, so that the seeds would germinate quickly, avoiding loss from birds.

Burning pastures was a fairly routine matter but could not be treated lightly. The pasture to be burnt was always tall grass and very dry, so that the flames would be extremely high and could spread very fast. Before a pasture was to be burnt the aceiro (fireguard) would be cleared. This was a strip of land on either side of the fence that was kept well cut, so that fire could not jump from one pasture to another. It also saved the fence posts from burning. The first area to be burnt was the down wind side, which is burnt back towards the centre. This is done if possible at a slow controlled pace, so that the fire slowly works up wind, thereby widening the fireguard. Winds are not always obedient and I have seen on more than one occasion, the wind change just as the down wind fires have been lit. Suddenly we have a raging fire hurtling towards the other side of the pasture. If the men at that end did not realise what had happened and act fast enough to burn back, a raging, wind swept fire can easily leap a fireguard and spread to the adjacent pasture. I have seen one fire leap the main farm road and blaze on through a pasture full of cattle.

Cattle have the sense to run from fire and usually few casualties occur but horses seem to lack this sense and can burn to death in an open field, frantically trying to kick the fire out instead of running away. I would never take Lindy anywhere near a pasture fire, because of the snakes that would wriggle out by the hundreds ahead of the flames. Many of these were the Rattlers, and, being already scared by the fire would go for anything in their way. I would occasional see a rattlesnake in the grass as I rode by but I soon learnt that they had no desire to attack me and would only bite cattle if they disturbed them while foraging for grass. A mother guarding her nest could be dangerous but otherwise they just wanted to be left alone.

I was out with the commitiva, on one of those tinderbox-dry days, where the grass and leaves seem to turn to parchment, when we noticed a tall column of smoke coming from inside the forest bordering the fazenda. It soon became clear that this was not just a campfire. In such dry conditions fires can start spontaneously. The trees soon became huge torches that could be seen for miles. Pearman was in Sao Paulo at the time so I had my moment of responsibility. With the extremely dry conditions the fire could spread rapidly and take a few pastures with it. It would be just my luck for Pearman to return and find half the farm ruined by fire. I rounded up some of the field workers and spent three exhausting days and nights in the forest trying to contain that fire. We didn't dare leave it, as a spread could be disastrous. If the wind, which was light, increased or changed directions we could be in bad trouble. We were able to circle the fire by the second day and slowly worked in towards the centre. The wind was still very light and I kept my fingers crossed that we would not get a sudden squall, which was not uncommon in the very hot climate. Sometimes as we moved on, a fire would suddenly spring up again behind us, where we had previously been satisfied that nothing was burning. This happened usually because a log or tree would be quietly smouldering inside. As the smouldering tree fell or the fire reached the other end of an already fallen log, a fire could break out again. This might happen even days after the fire was put out, so we left a man on watch for a week after the fire had finished.

We contained the fire by clearing firebreaks wherever we could, rather than try to beat the fire out. If we knew that a tree was smouldering we would cut it down and isolate it. There was of course no water in the immediate area.

I was able to get a few spells of sleep in the back of the jeep, which I had finally been given the use of, as I did not dare go home until the fire was well contained. Finally late into the third night, having combed the area for any more smouldering time bombs, I headed home, hungry, thirsty and dead tired.

When I struggled to the office the following day, Pearman was waiting for me with his eye of his watch. "What sort of time do you think this is for coming to work?"

"I have just spent the last three days fighting a forest fire." I protested. I got back at three this morning. Last night was my first night's sleep since the fire broke out."

"Is the fire out now?"

"I think so. I have left a couple of men up there for the moment to watch."

"Humph! Come into my office, I have some things for you to do." He turned and marched back into the office.

Besides cattle, we had a small herd of sheep, which we kept for consumption, as well as for their skins. The sheepskins were in great demand for saddle covers. They turn the very simple, bare Brazilian saddle into a comfortable seat. We also had a herd of wild pigs. I say wild although they were supposed to be domesticated. They were running around one of the big pastures that had been set aside for replanting. There was an enclosure for keeping them at night. This was the one I had been sent out to check on several months earlier. We were having quite a problem whenever we wanted to count the pigs or shut them in at night, so I decided to try the old Pavlovian trick of ringing a bell when the food was put in the trough. After a few days the message got through. The retireiro used this trick every night to get the pigs back in the enclosure. From then on, when I needed to count the pigs for a monthly check, all I had to do was ring the bell and stand back to avoid being trampled. I would arrive at the piggery, which was just a corral made by adjacent, upright aroeira (ironwood) posts and see perhaps one or two pigs honking around, otherwise nothing in sight. Once the bell had been rung the pasture came to life, hundreds of pigs appeared from every angle, running, jostling, squeaking and grunting in hysterical anticipation.

Every three months I would have to count the entire stock of the farm, just as I had done on other farms. It was essential to count a retiro within one day, so that there could be no overlapping. This required quite a bit of organisation. I would have to leave the house early in the morning, so as to get to the retiro before sunrise. The retireiro would have a horse ready for me and we would move out as the sun was rising. We usually had to ride a fair distance to our first rendezvous with the men, who had gathered the first herd at the furthest pasture so that we could work back to opposite end. The retiros were large and well stocked, so it would usually take all day; often ending up at the far end of the retiro, so that the ride back was mainly by moon-light. I would arrive at the house, sometimes at ten or eleven o-clock at night; almost time to start out for the next retiro.

On some occasions I had reason to spend a few days on a retiro and, rather than drive home each evening, I would stay over at the retiro for the night. There was no room for guests in the retireiro's house, so I just mucked in. As a rule I was offered a bed but somebody had to vacate it for me, so I would decline and just slept where I could. It was usually in a fairly small room, full of people. Retireiros like all other good Catholics, tended to have very large families. I could sometimes find myself in a room with all the sons, ranging from adult, down to quite young. The very young were usually in with the parents and the daughters. As a rule there were perhaps two or three beds, each containing one of the adults and one or two of the younger ones. The older boys would curl up and sleep wherever they could, using either a sheep's skin off one of the saddles, or a rice sack as a bed. There seemed to be no fixed position for anyone, and kids would tend to sleep where they dropped. With all these people clustered together, the air or at least oxygen tended to be in short supply. All the shutters were bolted shut so that not a breath of air could circulate. Usually I was so tired I fell into oblivion regardless.

It was decided that one of the retiros needed a new well, so a professional well digger was employed and the location chosen for the well. Whenever I was out that way I would take a moment to see how the well was progressing. Chico, the digger was a red haired, wiry man in his forties, who exuded both energy and a cheerful disposition. He just seemed to love his job. It was fascinating to watch Chico and his assistant at work. The well had to be quite deep before he would be able to find water and yet he did not reinforce the sides of the well at all. On the first day he walked around the proposed site and seemed to sense the right place to dig; he had no divining rods or other aids instead he just used his own senses. After choosing the spot, he cut a perfect circle on the ground and just started to gig.

As the well became deeper and Chico was no longer visible from the edge of the hole, his only contact with the surface was the rope attached to a bucket. The assistant never went down the well; instead he remained at the surface. He used the bucket to pull up the earth as it was dug out. I would sometimes lie down at the edge of the well and look down into the darkness below and could not see Chico working, even after giving my eyes time to adjust. I tried to follow the bucket down as it was lowered but lost visual contact long before the rope stopped moving. I looked at the unsupported walls and shuddered at the thought of what would happen if there were to be a cave-in. There would be no chance of rescuing the man, any attempt to dig him out, would just bring more soil down onto him. I asked Chico one day if he ever worried about that, he just laughed and said that he trusted his own skill.

Zebu cattle grazing.

30

A WALK IN THE PARK

When I was checking a pasture one day, I noticed that there was a broken strand of wire in one of the fences. I made a temporary repair and made a mental note to get it repaired. The following day I had nothing of great importance to do and the fence gang was otherwise engaged, so armed with a few feet of wire and a pair of pliers, I set off to repair the damage myself. It was a fair distance across several pastures, so I managed to take a look at some of the cattle on the way, as well as run my eye along the fences, each time I approached a gate.

Most of the gates out in the field are made with the two gateposts leaning slightly, so that the gate will always swing closed. It also makes it easier for a man on horseback, as his horse can push with his head to open the gate in one direction and it only requires pulling, without the necessity of unlatching, in the other direction. Cattle don't seem to cotton on to the gate opening techniques but horses learn from their rider, which makes it important to put a latch on any gate when there are horses in the pasture.

Sometimes horses become a little too eager to get through the gate, and while I was opening one gate, my horse pushed through, leaving me with one knee caught by the gate and the other by the gatepost. It was quite a painful encounter and cost me a pair of trousers. I continued on my way determined that at the next gate I would give my horse a little lesson in manners. As I opened the gate he pushed his head through and was about to repeat the previous exercise. I gave a sharp jerk on the reins, and, holding the gate well open, I made it clear that he should not move until the master gave the command. Feeling a little better, having regained the upper hand, I crossed the final pasture feeling once more at peace with the world, willing to forgive and forget: but not so my horse.

I found the break in the fence, so I dismounted and let the reins drop to the ground, which was the usual practice in the field. Cattle horses normally would not move from the spot where you drop the reins; it was an important part of their training and essential when you are out in the open field with nothing to tie them to. It did not take me very long to complete the repairs to the fence. Besides the broken strand some of the wire had been stretched where the cattle had pushed through. With the help of a stick I was able to create a loop and wind the strands tight again.

I was surprised when I turned back to remount, to find that my horse had wandered quite a few yards away. As I moved towards him, he moved away. I walked a little faster. He walked a little faster. I ran and so did he. I slowed down. So did my horse. He was heading back across the pasture, the way we had come.

"Get back here! Damn you" I yelled.

My horse stopped, looked back at me and bit off a tuft of grass. I foolishly took this for a sign and pushed forwards. He also pushed forwards.

"If you don't stop I am going to skin you alive!" Nothing!

"I am warning you!"

I cursed that horse and set off once more in pursuit, never getting closer than ten yards. It was a hot dry, windless day, with the heat shimmering off the scorched earth and the almost bleached grass. There was a long way to go before the next fence and gate, too far to even see at that point, as I trudged across the pasture with my horse just out of reach. I used every trick in the book, to no avail. At one point I stopped, and seeing that my horse had also stopped, I tried making cooing noises, with a forgiving, loving smile on my face.

"Come on boy, let's be friends. There's a good fellow."

That didn't work. I tried to hurt his feelings, by yelling every form of profanity that I could remember, in English or Portuguese, even threatening the knacker's yard. At the height of my hysteria he looked me straight in the eye and calmly took another mouthful of grass and munched it contentedly, with his gaze then fixed on a point just above my head.

"You are a bastard. You are going to be pulling a cart for the rest of your miserable life."

I was exhausted by the time we reached the fence. There was a soggy sweatband around my felt hat. The shirt was sticking to my back. My feet were blistered and on fire. The high cowboy boots that were useful for saving my legs from branches and gateposts, but were definitely not made for walking. With a fence between my horse and his destination I felt that finally I had him. I moved cautiously forwards.

"Don't you touch that gate now!" I pleaded, as I realized that he could push it open from this side.

The party was not over yet. The wretched horse trotted over and stood by the gate looking back at me waiting for me to catch up.

"Easy boy," I coaxed in a gentle loving way. "Wait for your beloved master."

I made a last concerted effort to grab him just before he blithely pushed the gate open and continued on his way. I was just in time to get the full weight of the five bar gate as it swung back into place.

"It's the knacker's yard for you." I screamed.

For a while I sat semi-stunned, hot, exhausted, bruised, offended and just plain old mad. I scanned the horizon hoping to see somebody but there wasn't a soul. There were a few steers standing idly nearby, watching the scene with mild interest. Through the bars of the gate I could see my horse, with a mouthful of grass watching me, with an arrogant, unsympathetic eye as he chewed.

"Why is this happening to me?" I asked the sky above me.

I set off once more ten yards behind my horse, not bothering to spurt, or coo, or yell, fully prepared to walk to the next fence, and then probably the next. The pastures were so vast that one fence disappeared long before the next one came into view. I felt that I was the only human being in an endless Brazilian landscape. It was beginning to edge towards evening, as the strange twosome trudged slowly towards the sede, with me still a mere ten yards behind, like Prince Phillip on a Royal walkabout. We came to the final gate; my mind now was a blank, I was beyond caring. I could see the sede perhaps half a mile further on, sloping down from the slightly higher ground that I stood on.

I trudged the last few feet towards the gate and paused, not wanting to be hit by a swinging gate. I found to my numbed surprise, that the hand that I had put out to push the gate open was met instead by the familiar leather of my saddle. My horse had made no effort to open that final gate. I grabbed the reins in triumph. At first my pent-up anger urged me to wreak my revenge and teach the beast a lesson. Instead I reached up and patted his neck and leant my head against his shoulder. At first my horse continued to ignore me but then turned his head and nuzzled it against my chest. I realized that he had spared me the shame and humility of returning to the sede, in torn trousers, walking ignominiously behind my horse.

There must have been a moral in the story somewhere though what I needed at that moment was not a moral but a long cool pull on a 'cerveija glace' (iced beer), some food and then, merciful sleep. But first I had to unsaddle my horse and then get swollen feet out of tight knee-length boots.

31

I DO THE CRIME AND DO THE TIME

Christmas on Jacaracatinga held no surprises. Mr. Pearman and family left for Barretos, leaving instructions that I was not to leave the farm while he was away. He also arranged for my jeep to be sent to Valparaiso, the nearest town, for 'essential' repairs. No work would be done on the jeep until the Christmas break was over but then pure logic did not enter into the equation. This was of course classic Pearman; every Saturday afternoon my jeep was taken for washing and greasing, which took the whole afternoon. I was therefore stranded and unable to join the others playing tennis or whatever. The timing was no accident, just malicious. Christmas Eve was a riot. I had given the cook the two days off for the holiday, so, with no transport, I spent the evening celebrating over some corned beef sandwiches and a bottle of beer, with Lindy as my only company.

Christmas day brought a little relief; one of the fruit people came up and drove me down to the Ederleys' house for a swim and some lunch. The Ederleys, he was the fruit manager, were a wonderful couple, and their house was always the centre of social life for the fruit expats and they went out of their way to make me feel equally welcome. They had no obligation to look after me, as I did not come under their wing; however they knew Pearman and took pity on me. I spent many a weekend with these warm and friendly people. During the entire time I was in Jacaracatinga, I only went to the Pearmans' house a few times, when he really had no option other than to include me and, as I have mentioned earlier, I lived to regret it. On Christmas night there was to be a dance at the Valparaiso social club, and the fruit bachelors were going in. After just a little persuasion I went with them. I allowed my conscience a little airing, as we left the farm but was soon enjoying the outing and the freedom.

The dance was just beginning when we got there; it was the usual rather stiff social affair with the boys and girls in self-conscious, embarrassed clusters, at the opposite ends of the hall. A few couples started to dance, bolt upright, scrupulously careful where they put their hands, and ever conscious of the never faltering eyes of the chaperones. We found a table and ordered a round of beers. The lunch party at the Ederleys' had stretched on a bit, and had not been entirely teetotal, so we were reasonably uninhibited already. A few dark glances had greeted us when we arrived, as we were known to be a little less refined than the local socialites and our attempts at securing partners were not very successful. By about eleven thirty we decided that the party needed a little livening up, so we found four toilet rolls and stationing ourselves at the four corners of the dance floor. We rolled them across the floor, causing pandemonium, with dancers thrashing about knee deep in the finest double layer bog paper. The four of us were curled up laughing, enjoying the best show of the year, happily oblivious to the complete lack of sense of humour around us. It was not long before we found ourselves being kindly yet firmly escorted outside, with nowhere to go. The nearest town of any description was Aracatuba, so we set off on the hundred odd kilometre journey to the Sete de Ouro nightclub in Aracatuba.

The club was situated in a rather shady area of town, on the edge of the red light district although the regulars amongst us knew it well. It was easy enough to find anyway as there was always a police camionette, 'Black Maria' and a few uniformed police hanging around outside. Inside the club the police had a permanent table with a sign 'POLICIA' prominently displayed on it. A poker faced cop sat glaring at the scene, never failing to bring the revellers back to reality, should they make unwanted passes, or start a fight. We had no trouble getting dancing partners here. Four well-endowed matrons soon zeroed in on us, and were soon helping us to spend our money—what little we had—with the occasional dance to wet our appetites.

I lost sense of time after a while. I was never a heavy drinker and I had definitely topped my limit and then some. Sometimes the room was going round, and I assumed that I must have been dancing, as a female face seemed to be the only thing not spinning. The poker face of the policeman kept coming into focus; his eyes seemed to be riveted on me. Sometimes the room settled down, and there was a table in front of me laden with drinks and surrounded by faces.

The overwhelming sounds of music and people hit me in waves. Finally I became aware that I was being led towards the door.

As we passed the police table, I had the desire to say goodnight to the nice policeman, however I noticed that the chair was empty. Only the 'POLICIA' notice glared at me. It looked so lonely I decided, purely out of compassion, to give it a home. Before I had time for a second thought, had I been able to have one, the lonely little notice was safely nestled inside my shirt and I was out of the club in the cool night air, being helped into the rear seat of the jeep. Murphy's law kicked in at this point: the jeep just would not start. We were all concentrating on the grinding of the starting motor and were not aware that we were surrounded and outnumbered. I became aware, through the haze, of blue uniforms, lots of blue uniforms, on either side of the vehicle. To the complete surprise of the other members of the party, we were all ordered out of the jeep and lined up. We stood, surrounded by surly policemen, with the sergeant eyeing each of us in turn.

"Quem tiro a noticia?" The sergeant demanded, as he brought his far from handsome face into to close proximity with each of ours. I was the last in the line, so by the time the sergeant got to me he was in no mood to mess with and I was just sober enough to realize it. Three people had looked him in the eye and sworn that they did not know what he was talking about. The sergeant kept screaming that the people in the club had seen one of us take the notice. I made a somewhat meek attempt at a smile, as I slowly slid the POLICIA notice from inside my shirt. I was just about to say "SURPRISE!" when I was grabbed from all sides and thrown bodily into the waiting police wagon.

Although I was sober enough to know what was going on, I was drunk enough not to really care. I sat in the back seat of the Black Maria and happily waved farewell to my three dumbfounded fellow revellers. I seemed to be watching the whole scene from the wings, in unconcerned amusement as someone else, who looked a lot like me, was trundled into the police station, booked, stripped of his belongings and thrown into the cooler. There were perhaps six other occupants in the cell, all completely oblivious of my arrival. I found a place on the floor amongst them and prepared to rest. My cellmates all appeared to be low life drunks in varying stages of inebriation. I wanted to explain to them that I did not belong here, it was all a mistake, but passed out before I could get my message across.

After some time, I had no idea just how long; I became aware of familiar voices along the corridor. My friends had apparently managed to get the jeep started and had turned up at the station to try to bail me out. The conversation seemed to go from a yelling match at first, to a coaxing, pleading approach and ending in obvious accord and the exchange of banter and finally the object of all this diplomacy was sprung. The police station seemed to be full of smiles as I was led out of the cellblock. Soon I had all my things back and was shaking the sergeant's hand. Everything was rosy until I asked the sergeant if he would let me keep the POLICIA notice for a souvenir. The expression on the sergeant's face changed abruptly but before anything else could happen, my companions frog-marched me to the jeep and we left town in a cloud of dust.

It dawned on me later as we were driving home, that had I not been released when I was, being the Christmas Holiday, I would have had to spend two days in that jail before seeing the magistrate. For a fellow who was not supposed to have left the farm, my presence in an Aracatuba police cell would have been a little difficult to explain.

This little episode might give you the impression that my life in the interior of Brazil was frequently punctuated by drunken orgies and general depravity in fact I rarely drank much, so that when I did I was quickly over my limit. Most young men celebrate their newfound manhood by trying to be manlier than the next guy and I certainly had a few of those moments. My first school reunion at St Edwards was one of those times. I met up with a group of contemporaries, each one trying to impress the other with his manhood and worldliness. We spent an evening, after the banquet, visiting the drinking establishments of Oxford. We finally piled into someone's car and returned to the room we had rented for the night. I had certainly reached my limit and gone beyond. I was sitting in the back seat of the car next to the left-hand door and, unbeknown to me, had left the tail end of my raincoat jammed in the door. On arrival at the boarding house my fellow back seat passengers exited from the right-hand door and I tried to follow them. Try as I would, I could not move from my side of the car. In hind sight there were two options open to me, I could have slid out of the rain coat and left the car, or, if there had been a single un-befuddled synapse still working in my brain, I could have opened the left-hand door and proceeded uninhibited, unfortunately neither option registered and so I settled back in the seat and passed out. In one of those rare times when someone missed me, my schoolmates returned to find out what had happened to me. The room that we were sharing had less bed space than our numbers warranted and I ended up sleeping fully dressed in my rented tuxedo from Moss Bros in the bathtub. I was woken some time the next morning by someone with a warped sense of humour, who turned on the bath tap. I luckily woke moments before drowning and had to explain to the Brothers

Moss, that I had been caught out in a heavy rainstorm that had not appeared on the weather map.

    My own real vice, as far as drink was concerned, was that cold bottle of beer at the end of a long, hot, dry day in the saddle. As my horse carried me home from a far pasture at the end of in the blazing sun, I longed for the feeling of the cold beer sliding down my throat. On arrival at home I would reach for a cold bottle of local beer and pour it into a tall glass. That first swallow, which would sometimes encompass the whole glassful, was pure ecstasy. If the first pull did not drain the glass, the remaining beer held no appeal to me; I might sip it later although often I just let it stand. I did not feel the urge to drink the evening or the weekend away as many of my colleagues did.

32

END OF AN ERA, SOME SOUL SEARCHING

A few weeks after my Christmas adventure in a Brazilian police cell, Mario Segundo, the usually quiet, reserved, office clerk returned from a business trip to Aracatuba. Mario was not a man that I would associate with impulse buying or gambling, yet he had bought an entire lottery ticket. Lottery tickets are sold in long sheets containing ten tickets with the same number. You can buy one tenth, a few tenths or the entire ticket. It is usually only the serious gambler who would buy the whole ticket, yet here was meek, mild Mario with a whole ticket. He explained that this was for the big one. There had been no winners for a while and the stakes had gone up to dazzling heights. Either through second thoughts or a little, or more likely a lot, of persuasion from his far from meek and mild wife, he had decided to offer a few of the tenths to whoever would buy them. I decided to help the poor man out and bought one.

The day for the big draw came and some lucky winner or winners took the huge prize. Our ticket did however have enough right numbers to give us consolation prize, which was a free ticket for the next draw. Of course the following draw was a small one, however to our utter amazement, we won. My tenth part of the winnings gave me the equivalent of several hundreds of pounds. It represented more money in one lump than I had ever seen let alone owned in my life, yet not enough to retire on.

My three-year contract was almost up. Soon I would return to England for leave and perhaps return for a further contract. I spent my last few weeks' soul searching. I rode round the farm seeing for perhaps the last time, the open pastureland—the foreverness of the Brazilian landscape—the cattle, content in their daily round of eating, drinking, sleeping and growing fat. When the time approaches to leave a place, as well as the people with whom one has worked, one tends to see them in a different light. I noticed people who I had taken for granted and realising that I may not see them again, which allowed my emotions to distort their place in my life. I found that I was already missing what I had not even consciously noticed before.

I cast my mind back over the eventful three years I had spent in Brazil. The days of discovery at Tres Barros held some of the most cherished memories and even today the thought of Brazil always leads to nostalgic memories of that first year. Everything was new and interesting, so different to anything I had known, before metamorphosing from an English greenhorn into a Brazilian cattleman. Mato Grosso, the wild country, stark and rather cruel, where I changed from boy to man: buried my faithful friend and constant companion Fred, and suffered from an ulcer: Sao Sebastiao, my convalescence posting, where I had the chance to blossom on my own and make a go of it. Barretos, socially great, the closest I came to a romantic encounter, where the work was demanding although mentally rather unchallenging.

Then my thoughts returned to Jacaracatanga, where I had wilted, wasting my last year going through the motions of assisting a man who wanted no assistance. Overall I knew that the three years had not been wasted. I had seen a part of the world that no twenty-day-see-the-world-excursionist would see and very few travellers of any kind would ever see. I had lived with, worked with, and learned from, the tough, rugged though immensely human Brazilian cattlemen. I had come to love these friendly folk, who could enjoy the same simple joke a hundred times, or could cry at the sight of a child in pain and yet knew death as a normal part of life. I had almost become a Brazilian. I could speak their language as they spoke it; I could even think in the language. I could almost follow a football radio commentary, which I can hardly do in English.

I had to make a decision. It was not a very easy one to make. I was still only twenty-four, single with no strong attachments in England; Penny's letters had become fewer and further between as well as appearing to have been written out of duty rather than desire. One day, I must assume, I would have a family and so I focused my attention on the managers and their families. I had met many of them on some on the farms I had worked on and others at Barretos, or at the annual farms' weekends at Tres Barros, where the expat farm people would congregate for a weekend of partying. Most of the men were normal hard working people, with an interesting and absorbing job. Some of them drank heavily. Some became a bit peculiar, either introvert and suspicious, like Mr. Pearman or otherwise a bit weird.

It was the wives that made me wonder most of all. A few of the wives had adapted well to farm life and became involved in some way, or devoted their time to the children and the house and garden. Many became bitter, or eccentric, or drank themselves into a state of euphoria. Others just could not take it any longer and left. Children, if they were at boarding school, came out from England only once a contract. There were usually no shops or theatres, or even other English women to talk to within miles. Many of the marriages had broken up under the strain. Some managers had, often reluctantly, had to leave Brazil to save their marriage, just when they were getting their own farm or moving on to a bigger one.

I decided that I needed to talk to someone, so I drove over to the nearest neighbouring, company farm. Kelvin, the manager was a young man, who I had met on several occasions in various parts of Brazil. He, a bachelor like me, had also been moved about quite a lot. This was his second contract, and he had finally been given his own farm to run. It was Sunday, and I drove for three hours over bad, seldom used roads to reach his house. As I arrived at the sede I found myself in a delightful, picturesque, old-world setting. The manager's house was set on one side of a square that was occupied on the other three sides by unusually charming, old, wooden sede buildings and corrals, interspersed and partially hidden by huge mature figueiro trees. It was an old long established farm that had the feeling of changeless history. It was quiet around the sede as I drove in, though I did not need to ask directions; I had recognized Kelvin's jeep parked outside his bungalow. The manager's bungalow was set back a little from the main sede square, surrounded by a rather faded, white, picket fence, which enclosed a small, mature, although obviously well tended garden. The ivy covered walls and potted plants that decorated the traditional, wide, open veranda, blended and became a part of the garden.

I had had no way of announcing my pending arrival, so my entrance was totally unexpected. I clapped my hands as I approached, as was the custom. There was no response and there seemed to be no signs of life. I called Kelvin's name loudly and discretely entered the house. A rather blurry voice finally greeted me from another section of the veranda. I was horrified to find my colleague in a state of inebriated befuddlement. It was barely lunchtime and he was sitting there, one hand on a well-depleted bottle and the other barely holding a glass, drinking himself into a stupor. There wasn't much I could do for the poor fellow. I stayed with him for a while, trying to make some form of conversation and then as he finally passed out, I made him as comfortable as I could, and diplomatically left him to it. I doubt that he even knew that I had been there.

My plans to sound my colleague out about the future came to nothing. Kelvin had decided a year previously to return for the second contract and I wanted to hear his views, get his reassurance, or perhaps advice. All my fears of isolation and loneliness returned in that short visit. His lack of ability to advise me was advice in itself. I had never been a lone drinker, however many of the farm people had turned to the bottle in their isolation. This visit to my neighbour was perhaps the final blow that tipped the scales. I decided to join the many people before me who had done one contract and not returned. It was not an easy decision to make and many have been the times since, when I have hankered for fazenda life—the clear skies, pure streams, the simple life as nature intended it. I have looked back at those years and yearned for the quiet, rural peace, interspersed with the occasional excitement and the fulfilment of it all.

My last night on the farm saw the noisiest, rowdiest group of people, drinking local liquor until they were stoned out of their minds. They were the coffee bachelors, Jonathan, the young addition who was to take over my job, and my neighbour Kelvin. I did not mention the visit I had made a few weeks before and neither did Kelvin. When the driver came for me the next morning, he had to walk me round the room until I was semiconscious. First he had to move some of my guests, so we had enough room to walk. I cannot in all honesty say that I left Jacaracatinga experiencing any deep emotion; I was feeling very sick, calling upon the driver to stop on several occasions to prove my point. Leaving Lindy behind was my only real regret. Luckily Jonathan, my replacement, loved dogs and he and Lindy hit it off. At least I knew that she still had a place to stay. Lindy had been a wonderful companion, not as intelligent as Fred, but more gentle and loving; I definitely missed her.

I was booked on the Paraguay Star, the same ship that I had travelled in overnight with my mother. She was a much bigger ship than the Debrett that I had travelled out on and carried many more passengers. It was a pleasant journey back and I felt ready to face the uncertain future as we neared the end. It was of course raining as we docked in Southampton, two weeks after leaving Rio, after a very rough passage across the Bay of Biscay, two very near collisions in thick fog in Le Havre and more fowl weather in the English Channel. England, to my observation had not changed very much, the Conservative government under Anthony

Eden had given way to a Conservative government under Harold Macmillan; the sky was still grey and the streets greyer. January! What a month to return to England in, it certainly brought me back to reality. For three years I had been writing to Penny, my childhood girlfriend. We met in London the following day. At first Penny seemed to be the same girl that I had left three long years before. I soon realized however, that not only had she changed, after three years learning to be a physiotherapist in a London Hospital, and being involved in the social whirl of South Kensington in the fifties, but I also had changed. The bustle of London and the social pace of the South Ken singles was a shock to my nervous system. I found that after an hour at one of those high-decibel, low-ventilation, 'just-everybody-was-there,' parties, and I was fighting for space, air and, most of all, quiet. I was starting to regret my decision already. Oh God! Just to be able to go out in the sunshine again, feeling the heat on my face and the rhythm of my horse, smell that honey sweet smell of the cattle, surrounded by endless space.

The Paraguay Star leaving Rio de Janeiro.
A painting by Robert G. Lloyd.

EPILOGUE

♦

THE YEAR 2000

We had spent the day standing on the back of a pick-up truck, fitted with railings to hold on to, like a pre-terrorism Pope Mobile, while the driver took us for a tour of part of Fazenda Estrela. Rod Paxton, Richard Turnley and I reviewed thousands of acres of pasture and huge herds of home-reared cattle. There were heifers and steers from various crosses with European cattle and they all seemed to be thriving on the wonderful African grasses. I had to pinch myself to make sure that I was really back in Ligacao, as I knew it, now known as Estrela. Although it was greener and cleared of much of the scrub trees, it brought back such vivid memories from so many years ago. A time so long ago that I had sometimes wondered if that whole adventure had not just been a figment of my imagination; yet here it was before my very eyes.

Wild life seemed to be all the more conspicuous, probably because of the openness of the pastures. Rheas, often in little families ran from the noise of the truck, although luckily not too far for me to see them and of course photograph them. The Seriema (Secretary birds) scampered busily amongst the grass. A sound like the honking of startled geese came from the Curicacas, (Spider birds) as they took to flight in protest against our unwanted presence. The Curicacas have long flexible beaks that served them well for reaching into holes in search of spiders and other insects.

One animal that I had hoped to see again although sadly did not was the Tamandua Bandeiro, the Giant Anteater. These are the big, slow-moving, hairy animals with the distinctive long nose and striped body that ends in a huge bushy tail, that I remembered seeing making their lumbering rounds of the large termite hills that dotted the property. This beautiful animal is fast becoming one of the endangered species. Luckily here on Estrela and Lageada, my next destination, they were treated with respect and left alone.

The three of us met out on the veranda as the sun sank for another night of rest. Rod brought out some cold beers as we sat, enjoying the cool evening breeze. At the end of the garden, beyond the gate, that was framed by a huge arched Bougainvillaea, was my previous house—dark and deserted now and rarely used—it's presence still caused long forgotten images to flicker before me.

"Of course this house was not built when you were here, Bruce." Rod was talking about the house we were sitting outside. "It was started by Peter Richardson, your old manager, although he never lived in it."

"Yes, I thought it was different. The old house used to be further towards the office."

"Yes, the old foundations are still there. We can walk over there tomorrow."

"What happened to the airstrip?"

"Most of the old private airstrips are gone now." Rod explained. "The government set up some pretty stringent rules for private airstrips and as roads improved it was not worth the expense of upgrading and applying for permits and so on. Most people just turned them back to pasture."

The conversation turned to people I might have known and what had become of them.

"Peter Richardson died at quite a young age. His wife, Shirley still lives in Brazil," Richard informed me. I was sorry to hear that Peter had died; he had been a good and decent manager, although I saw little of him because of his frequent buying trips.

"One person you must have met at some time is Douglas Mackenzie. He is still around, well over ninety and still hail and hearty."

"Was he a cattle buyer?" I asked, trying to recall the name. "He used to live and work from Ribeirao Preto, if that is the man I am thinking of."

"That's him," Richard confirmed. "He came out in the late twenties and helped to open up some of the earliest farms."

"He opened up Mutum, here in Mato Grosso," Rob added.

"I did meet him a few times, I remember, the most vivid memory I have of him was when I was on Jacaracatinga, under that bastard Pearman. Doug Mackenzie, not being one to trust the Brazilian postal service, used to pass over the office in his *Teko Teko* and drop cattle purchase notes, wrapped in a stone. He would some times be flying so low that I could see the whites of his eyes."

"Let's call him. I am sure that he would like to chat with you. He has an amazing memory for his age and loves to talk to the old hands."

Rod brought out the cordless telephone and dialled the number. I felt a little nervous, as I was sure that he would not have remembered me. I was very junior at the time and Doug Mackenzie was already one of the company's legends.

Douglas came on the line and Rod talked to him for a while, he then explained that he had someone staying with him who had known him forty odd years ago. "His name is Bruce Vaughan. He knew you when he was on Jacaracatinga. He would like to say 'hello' to you." Rod passed the phone to me.

"I don't expect you to remember me, I was Assistant to Pearman and I remember you circling the office in your plane to deliver cattle documents."

"Oh yes, I think we also met in Barretos." I was impressed.

"You did a lot of flying in those days."

"Absolutely: I did thousands of miles in that plane, always with the same pilot. Would you believe it? That plane is still going strong today although the pilot is dead now."

We talked for a few more minutes. Doug asked about my life since Brazil. I gave him a quick summary, then I handed him over to Richard who knew him very well and they chatted for a while.

As the evening wore on we talked of Tres Barros, where Richard had been manager. He had been there when the decision had been made to turn it over to sugar.

"As a cattleman, that must have broken your heart." I ventured.

"At first, yes but then I became quite caught up in the sugar business and found it really fascinating."

"It was a lovely old estate. The sede along with the manager's house was something out of *Gone with the Wind*. I'll never forget my first day, being driven by DP through the covered gateway into the sede square. It was as if I had travelled back in time. None of my preconceived images came anywhere close to that first impression."

"That is all still there: even the old water wheel. Head office wanted to get rid of it at one time but I protested strongly and they backed down." Richard recalled. "It gave a wonderful old-world atmosphere, sitting as it did just next to the old slave house, which has recently been designated as an historic building."

"I remember that. You could still see the metal rings that they used to shackle the slaves with at night." I was wallowing in rich memories.

"There was one old guy who claimed that he had been a slave, still working there when a I was there." Richard said as he topped up my glass. "He was very old yet he was happy doing a few simple jobs until he died a few years after I took over." The faint sound of a train broke the silence of the evening.

"I remember DP pointing him out to me. He looked pretty old even then."

"We must take Bruce to Ribas do Rio Pardo tomorrow, Richard. The passenger trains that you remember don't run any more; they haven't for many years now. There were outbreaks of various diseases that seemed to be spreading along the course of the railway. The outbreaks were blamed on Paraguay, where the trains come from, so they closed the border for passengers. They just haul freight now."

"Is the Ligacao station still there?" I asked.

"Yes, the old station is there although very run down. We can stop there on the way to Rio Pardo."

"That would be great. I spent many hours there, either waiting for trains or loading cattle. We used Ligacao for the cattle that were being held in the pastures around the sede or the western pastures. The ones that came from the eastern end of the farm or Cervo were loaded in Rio Pardo," I said. "So I got to know both stations pretty well."

"You mentioned someone by the initials DP earlier when we were talking about Tres Barros. Who was that?" Richard asked.

"Bernard Dupont," I replied." He was a Frenchman, though born and raised in Brazil. He was the cattle section manager and my immediate boss. He left the company just before I left Tres Barros."

"That was way before my time. I did not come out here until the seventies." Richard said. "Rod came out at about the same time."

"Yes, that's right. I finished my degree in agriculture and then joined Vesteys."

"There must have been a mega change in policy. They used to have the notion that it is better to send someone out with no farming experience and train him on the job, than to have to un-train him of the British farming concepts before retraining him with Brazilian concepts."

"Yes, that was the old idea but Brazil was fast coming into the twentieth century and the company realized it."

It seemed strange, sitting there on the manager's veranda after all these years. The house, although different from the one I had know on the few occasions when I had been a guest there, was a pleasant bungalow with a simple but spacious and well-kept garden surrounding a fair sized swimming pool. There was one big change in the life of the farm managers. When I had been there, both the managers and assistants were hired on an all-found basis. Salaries were reasonably low, because housing, servants and food were provided by the company. As an assistant, the manager carefully monitored my expenses on the company's account, many of the managers provided for themselves a little bit too well. The Company finally did away with the all-found contracts and raised the salaries slightly. Rod Paxton had a part time servant, who came in daily. Richard had cooked the evening's dinner, with a little help from Rod and encouragement from me.

On our way back from the airport, Rod and I had spent twenty minutes at the super-market buying supplies. I was surprised to see milk butter and meat in the shopping cart. We had been able to support ourselves off the farm. I mentioned this to Rod.

"Times have changed," Rod explained, "the authorities won't allow us to kill our own meat and the company decided not to keep dairy herds for the staff. We just go to the supermarket like everyone else."

We spent the following day covering every corner of Fazenda Estrela and also made a detour to Ribas do Rio Pardo, stopping on the way at the Ligacao station. It was like a forgotten film lot from a movie company that had been left behind. There was no sign of the corrals and ramps where we loaded cattle. The station building, that had been the pride of my friend the stationmaster, was in a sorry state of repair. Mature weed trees grew from cracks in the building and the roof had partly caved in. The sign on the wall still stood proudly announcing to all comers that this was 'Ligacao, Alt 457' (metres). We made another small detour before Rio Pardo, to the next station called Arlindo Luz. This could have been where the would-be politician had made his last pitch. Arlindo Luz's once proud structure is also sadly abandoned, except for a family of squatters. The head of the family, a rather thin yet healthy looking old man, was happy to invite us in to his 'property' and show us around. He had spent his working life driving large trucks but now, in retirement he and his wife had moved in to the abandoned station. He proudly showed us the water tower that had been hit by a train and was leaning quite precariously. The wagons from the wrecked train were still there, shunted into a siding and left to rot. I was amazed at how narrow the rail tracks were; more like what you would find in a theme park. .

Ribas do Rio Pardo is now a flourishing town. The road leading off from the highway passes block after block of urban spread. Factories, shops, schools and offices are criss-crossed by well-kept avenues and streets. At the bottom of the hill we met the railway track once more and there, looking as sad as the others, stood the station building on the old main street. The houses across the street looked very similar to the ones I remember but they are now very definitely on the wrong side of the track. One of those houses could have been the old inn where I stayed.

One of our trips took us out to Pontal and Cachoeira where Sebastiao had died. What was barely more than a track then is a passable road now, and the round trip, with a few stops took us only a few hours. We crossed the little stream Agua Limpa, and Richard reminded me of the legend that once you have drunk the water from the stream, you will always return. I had drunk from the stream several times and had indeed returned after forty-two years. The pastures, all the way out to Pontal, are clear now. They are stocked with fat and healthy cattle that have been bred and reared on Estrela.

We stopped at the river where I had found Sebastiao. Years of floods and dry spells have changed the course of the river somewhat although the waterfall was there, just as I remembered it. I stood near the deep pool below the fall and remembered the laughter as saddle weary cowboys turned into kids, splashing and dunking, or just standing under the water as it washed away the dust and heat of the day.

On our way back we passed a hydroelectric dam that had had its time and now waited for nature to take it back to her fold. Rod asked me if it had been there back then in 1958. I could not remember having seen it. Our driver reckoned that it had been built in the early sixties. So it had been built, lived out its useful life and now lay nearly hidden by the trees and almost forgotten, between my two visits to Brazil.

My short though emotional visit to Estrela came to an end all too soon. I packed my bags once more and put them into the back of Rod's pick-up for the journey to Lageada, where I was to spend my last two and a half days in Mato Grosso. Rod, Richard and I set off for Campo Grande for lunch at a popular Churasscaria. The churasscaria comes from Rio Grande do Sul and has gradually become popular throughout Brazil. We were seated at a small table near the window. Rod explained that there was a salad bar in the centre of the restaurant and we went over to fill our plates. What happened next was what made the churasscaria different. As we sat at the table waiters kept arriving with large cuts of rotisserie cooked meats still on the spit, and carved off portions for us. In some restaurants, each customer is given what looks like a place mat, green on one side and red on the other. If you don't want them to bring any meat for the moment, you turn the red side upwards. When you are ready for more you turn the green side upward. The waiters just kept coming until we finally said enough and called for the bill.

Our lunchtime conversation was a continuation of several before in which we reminisced about old times. I mentioned Sao Sebastiao, the banana plantation where I had started a dairy herd. Rod and Richard exchanged glances.

"Is Sao Sebastiao still part of the company?" I asked.

"No," Richard answered. "Back in the late sixties there was a disastrous flash-flood that took half the company's land, including most of the bananas, which, as you will remember, were on the lowest part of the land. The company decided to just walk away from Sao Sebastiao, selling what was left."

"What a terrible shame. It was a beautiful spot." I could just see that innocent little river that I had waded across on horseback suddenly devouring hundreds of acres of banana groves.

"David Harrison, the manager at the time, was in UK on leave. He caught a glimpse of his estate being washed out to sea, on the television news one night." Rod recalled. "Poor guy, he knew then that he would have no job to come back to."

"I remember David," I said. "He was the senior assistant when I was there and I had known him on Tres Barros for a month or so after I first arrived. He was a very serious and ambitious guy; I remember his excitement when he was first posted to Sao Sebastioa. There had been some misunderstanding as he thought that he was being posted there as manager whereas it was to be as manager in charge of a new division only."

"Well he got the job eventually when Braham retired. When the flood hit, the company just paid him off, packed up his personal property and sent it back to him in the UK. It was all very abrupt; poor guy."

"It must have broken his heart." I said, as I pictured the idyllic dream job that he waited so long to get, washed away within a matter of hours.

We passed through Campo Grande once more, before heading out toward Lageada. I noticed the large store named Casas Pernambucanas. It is a large chain of stores that, according to Rod, had over reached its self and was now in serious financial trouble.

"That name is embedded on my brain," I noted. "Almost every gate along any route around Campo Grande had a small sticker that merely said 'Casas Pernambucanas,' I had no idea, for a long time what they referred to and yet it was beaten into my memory."

"The power of advertising," laughed Richard.

The drive from Campo Grande along the new interstate highway is virtually a straight run for miles. I had made the journey by train and plane when I had been there before. Travelling by road had not been a viable option then; even going in to Campo Grande was a major undertaking. I had enjoyed the two days on Fazanda Estrela, I was getting used to the name, not Ligacao as I remembered it and felt sad to leave it so soon.

After an uneventful drive along the interstate, we turned off onto a side road that soon became a more familiar earth road that would lead us to Fazenda Lageada. We passed the small village Palmeiras and crossed the railway, where I had, all those years before boarded the train after visiting the Fazenda.

"The property used to extend this far," Rod explained. "But the company did a land deal with the contractors who cleared the land. Instead of money, they got a percentage of the land after clearing the bushes." It would have been a massive undertaking, I realized; the now clean pastures were in stark contrast to the semi jungle of the past. It was a good half an hour's drive from the interstate to the sede. The landscape was quite stunning, with granite peaks rising out of the lush green. One particular pair was the favourite of the local male population. From certain angles the granite peaks clearly resembled the breasts of a reclining woman. Many mature trees still remained and some areas were kept as nature reserve. We were occasionally able to see, in the far distance through the trees, the huge escarpments that bordered the fazenda on three sides. From the entrance road they were merely distant features on the horizon, but became more impressive the further we travelled.

When we arrived at the sede Rod introduced me to my new host, Elisiario Cleto de Oliveira. My heart sank when I realized that he did not speak a word of English and my Portuguese was more than a little rusty after all those years. Elisiario has been with the company for close to twenty years and been the manager of Lageada for six of those years. Elisiario, in his late forties, is a tough, no nonsense and capable, Brazilian administrator. He was also a very amiable person, with a ready smile, accentuated by his grey streaked beard and great sense of humour. His rapid, somewhat staccato Portuguese was frequently punctuated laughter.

Rod told Elisiario that my most vivid memory of Lageada was the jungle area that I had spent a day riding through. Elisiario pointed to one of the distant escarpments and told me that that was where I had ridden and he would drive us all there. After a pause at the house to leave my bags, we all set off for the far border of the fazenda to revisit my jungle. It was a beautiful drive. We were able to see the various escarpments that formed the border in front of us and on either side. The largest and most dramatic of the rock faces was where we were heading. It remained a prominent part of the scenery throughout the forty-five minute drive. As we had left the house, Rod mentioned the airstrip, recalling where it had been as he pointed to on area just beyond the manager's house.

"That doesn't seem right to me," I replied, a little confused. "I remember landing right down near the office." The new manager's house was a fair distance from the office. Rod conveyed my confusion to Elisiario.

"Yes, that would be right. The original strip came down parallel to the stream, ending at the road to the sede and the old manager's house." We drove past there later in the day.

A large family of Rheas crossed the road and ran into the grass; there must have been about a dozen of them, including a few young. The birds were clearly not too afraid of us but kept a respectable distance. We stopped for a moment to watch them, and I, acting like the tourist, took a few pictures. The beautiful, lush, new pastures spread before us as we continued our drive. Herds of well-fed, clean and contented cattle continued their rhythmic chewing, as they watched us pass. A pair of Blue Macaws flew above us, circled and settled into a tree. We arrived at the retiro, nestled at the edge of the remaining jungle with the high, sheer face of the escarpment giving a dramatic backdrop. I was glad to see that there was still plenty of the jungle left. Part of the area that had been virgin jungle when I had ridden through it, is now beautiful open pasture. There was however a large section of jungle left at the foot of the escarpment.

After a fascinating tour of one section of the fazenda, that took us through both new pasture as well as old—more like the landscape that I had known in the past—to corrals full of cattle being vaccinated and branded, we returned to Elisiario's house. In the delicious cooling of the evening, as the sun showered its last red, orange and golden rays across the sky, we sank our tired and dusty bodies into the clear water of the manager's pool. Servants kept our glasses primed with cold beer and placed bowls of nuts by the poolside, while four cattlemen, both past and present, enjoyed good company. As the last rays of sunlight faded, a new moon stood clear above the distant escarpments. The air was so clear that the entire moon was visible, like a giant orange with just one edge picked out by a backlight from the retreating sun. There was a delicious stillness in the air as the Mato Grosso countryside settled down for another night.

It was with a genuine regret that I bade my two departing hosts from Estrela farewell. I could not have been treated with more kindness and respect if I had been Lord Vestey himself. Rod and Richard still had a long drive through the night, back to Fazenda Estrela.

Although my memories of Lageada were not so clear as they were for Estrela (Ligacao), as I had only paid fleeting visits in the fifties, my two days spent there were most enjoyable. Elisiario and his wife were wonderful hosts and made me feel part of the family. The following day I awoke early and went with Elisiario to the office for the start of the day. The early morning in Mato Grosso has a special charm. The air is crisp and sometimes quite cold as the sun makes long shadows over the endless landscape. We drove over to one of the retiros where they were vaccinating the cattle. I stood at the shoot, as I had done countless times in the past, and watched the frightened steers being funnelled through the narrow long wooden passageway, where they could be held almost motionless, whilst being vaccinated and then separated by gates that could direct them one way or another. Some of the steers were also being branded with the same company brand that I had known. It is in the shape of an '&'.

We returned to the house for a very Brazilian breakfast of rice and beans, some beef and pork and of course, coffee. We then took a long circuitous drive to another part of the farm, some areas of which were still un-cleared, with poor native grass, mature trees and dense undergrowth. Cattle could sometimes be glimpsed hidden amongst the bushes; they were the hardier Zebu strains of cattle, rather than the now more familiar mixed breeds. This was much more like the Lageada that I remembered.

In the afternoon, Elisiario had to go into Aquidauana, a town a few hours drive away, on the edge of the Pantanal. He had to attend a hearing there concerning a labour dispute. As we were leaving the farm we encountered a large boiada spread out along the part of the road that also served as a public cattle trail. There must have been about five hundred head of cattle. They were several days into a long trail that passed through Lageada. We slowly edged our way through the cattle with the help of the capitaz, who rode ahead of us, shushing the cattle out of our way. He was the only man I saw during this trip to Mato Grosso wearing a gun; in my days everyone wore a gun.

"Guns have to be registered," Elisiario explained. "A boiada capitaz has a good reason for a gun and providing he is well respected he can get a gun registered."

We stopped for lunch at another Churasscaria; a little more rustic than the one Rod and Richard had taken me to in Campo Grande. We sat overlooking the river as the waiters came running from table to table offering choice pieces of meat. Frankly I found the meat rather tough nevertheless I enjoyed the atmosphere and filled up on the salad. Neither of us wanted to drink beer in the middle of the day and I was delighted to get reacquainted with a local soft drink called guaraná, a very popular Brazilian drink made from a tropical herbal plant with small red fruit, it has a high caffeine-content. The fruit is found in the Amazon region, where the natives chew the seeds for energy. I remember guaraná from the first time I visited Brazil as a boy. It was my favourite drink; my mother's was rum and guaraná.

As we relaxed by the river after the meal, I noticed a sight that I had seen just a few times before. It was a tiny hummingbird hovering at the mouth of a flower, just a few feet from where I sat. I am sure that it was a Brazilian Amethyst; the smallest bird you can imagine. The wings were just a blur as it hung in mid air and then darted to another flower. I had seen a few of these amazing little birds during my stay in Brazil. I am not a botanist but had I been as interested in wild life as I am today I would have made better use of my three years in Brazil.

As we returned to Lageada we again passed through the small village of Palmeiras, where yet another station lies abandoned. As I have mentioned this had been my gateway to Lageada on the few occasions in the past when I had travelled there by train. We met the boiada once again, this time further into the fazenda. Boiadas move at such a very leisurely pace, they would probably have taken another full day to pass through Fazenda Lageada.

One of the directors of a cattle-feed company from Montana in the States, along with his local manager, came to review some cattle that they were sponsoring. The Montana Company had been involved in creating a breed of cattle called Montana. A small herd was held on Lageada and some of the heifers were to be exhibited at an upcoming agricultural show. Early the following morning, my last day in Mato Grosso, I joined the group as they headed off to inspect the cattle. We arrived at a retiro about half way towards the escarpment, where the cattle had already been assembled. They were a beautiful group of about fifty, two and three year old heifers. The people from Montana walked amongst them looking for the best. Gradually thirty of the most beautiful were separated out and then branded with a double Montana running **'M'** brand. One 'M' was inverted under the other.

After the Montana people left, Elisiario took me for the final drive up to a high point that had an almost uninterrupted view of the entire estate. The escarpments, miles apart, stood as thin ribbons, reflecting the morning's sun, forming the horizon as well as the boundaries of Lageada. Lageada certainly earns its place as the most beautiful of the company's fazendas. With the newly cleared land and imported grass it has become a showpiece. I felt privileged to have been given the chance to visit the fazenda, not just as a casual visitor but also with full VIP treatment, as had also been the case in Estrela.

At the end of my week long trip down memory lane, Elisario dropped me at Campo Grande Airport, bidding me farewell with the admonition "nao esquerco as gente," meaning don't forget people. He and his family had made me feel genuinely and unreservedly welcome during my few days on Fazenda Lageada. As I passed through the passengers' entry, I stepped once more alone into the impersonal bustle of twenty first century air travel, only to be greeted from across the boarding lounge by a hearty wave and a friendly smile. The man from the Montana Company was just about to board an earlier flight.

As the Varig Airbus rose into the evening sky I had a tremendous feeling of satisfaction at having re-visited a part of my life that had become so remote as to have left me in doubt as to its reality. There had been occasions on which I had mentioned my Brazilian cowboy days to acquaintances, when I had felt the same incredulity that I was witnessing in my audience. Had it all been just a wild fantasy, triggered by a book or a film? This trip was to convince me, no one else and it certainly had. It is so often a great mistake to go back. The present is never the same as the memories of the past and indeed today's Mato Grosso is a very different place to the one I had known. The one horse town Campo Grande of those days is now a bustling modern city.

The straight, wide, tar macadam road that had taken us to the entrance to Fazenda Estrela is a far cry from the treacherous, sandy or muddy, tortuous track that it was in the fifties. Both Estrela and Lageada, are now clear, lush, high yielding, open pastureland, rather than the poor scrubland that I had known. In spite of these changes both places are still essentially the places I remember. Life for the farm people is however very different today, with good roads, cable television, computers and that indispensable invention the Internet. Amongst all this modernisation however, the Brazilian cowboy hasn't really changed; the boots and spurs, the butcher's knife slipped into the belt, sheepskin covered saddles and lassos are all still just the way I remembered them. The honey sweet smell of Zebu cattle packed into a corral triggered a hundred memories, as did the clear, clean, endless Brazilian sky.

There have been very few times in my life when I have felt and knew that I felt, real happiness at the time it was happening but I had just spent a week knowing that I was experiencing one of those rare and wonderful periods of happiness. In my mind Brazil had become such a dim, illusive memory over the previous four decades, like a black and white movie vaguely recalled, that it was such a joy to see it once more in living colour and hear the sounds, smell the smells and just sense the great, up country out-doors.

Had it been a mistake to go back?

I knew without any doubt that it had not. It had been a satisfactory closure, not to a bad memory but a good one that had dimmed with time.

I left Campo Grande with a pleasant buzz in my head. I had gone back and it had been good. So often going back shatters the memories and spoils the images one has of a time and place gone by. Mato Grosso was different, even unrecognisable in some ways yet the sheer joy of going back to the wide-open spaces and familiar landscape overshadowed the differences and in many ways reinforced the most pleasant memories.

As the modern jet climbed high over the ageless Mato Grosso landscape my mind reluctantly returned to the present. I was on my way to join my colleagues on the Council of the World Federation of Chiropractic, for our meeting at the University of ASPEUR-Feevale University in Novo Hamburgo, Rio Grande do Sul, that coincided with the first graduation ceremony of Chiropractors in Brazil. During the twelve years of my involvement since the beginning of WFC, I had been able to take a break from my practice in Hong Kong and journey to many different countries where we held our annual Council meetings and biannual Assemblies. I had been delighted to know that Brazil had been chosen for the year 2000. My subsequent election at the end of the Council meeting, as the President of the WFC, was for me the icing on the delicious cake of my return to Brazil, after an absence of more than forty years.

The author with Rod Paxton (left), Fazenda Estrela.

On a Pope-mobile with Elisiario, Fazenda Lageada.

Adeus Amigo

Bruce Vaughan provides an entertaining and informative overview of Brazilian cattle ranching during the fifties. This is one man's personal journey from the British Army to the open ranges of a foreign country. Here and throughout, the author provides essential hooks that keep me engaged as a reader. As readers, we follow the author as he learns Portuguese and adapts to a different culture and way of life. We learn the ins and outs of milking, herding cattle, branding and lassoing. The author takes us on a wide array of adventures—he takes the reader right into the heart of the scene or conversation without unnecessary cluttering or set-up. From the beginning, he has me literally hooked. iUniverse editor.

"I was enraptured by the excitement, the humour and the pathos of this ascinating book. I absolutely feel as though I've been to Brazil."
Aileen Bridgewater, MBE, writer, broadcaster.

ABOUT THE AUTHOR

Bruce Vaughan left Brazil to become a rubber planter in Malaya, as it was then and then at the age of twenty-eight went back to school and earned a Doctor of Chiropractic Degree. He now lives in Hong Kong where he practices as a chiropractor. This is his third book.

Photographs and Artwork supplied by the author.

0-595-32421-5

Printed in the United Kingdom
by Lightning Source UK Ltd.
102328UKS00002B/283-309